BUSES

Yearbook 1998

Edited by
STEWART J. BROWN

IAN ALLAN
Publishing

Contents

British Bus — A Rough Ride
Stephen C. Morris 3

Nottingham Lions
Roy Marshall 20

Highland Holiday
Mark Bailey 25

Brief Revivals
Peter Rowlands 32

Transports of Delight
Gavin Booth 43

Lost Soulmates
Alan Millar 50

Going, Going, Almost Gone...
Stewart J. Brown 61

Bristol Fashion
Kevin Lane 73

North from Enfield
Simon Butler 80

Which Way Forward?
Michael H. C. Baker 83

Joy Ride
John Aldridge 92

Twenty-year Gap
Michael Fowler 93

Some Open-toppers I Have Known
Martin S. Curtis 97

When Duple was Dominant
Geoff Mills 105

Schools
Robert E. Jowitt 111

Nottingham in the Nineties
David Barrow 119

The Other Highland
Alistair Douglas 122

First published 1997

ISBN 0 7110 2527 4

All rights reserved. No part of this book may be reproduced or transmitted in any form or by any means, electronic or mechanical, including photocopying, recording or by any information storage and retrieval system, without permission from the Publisher in writing.

© Ian Allan Ltd 1997

Published by Ian Allan Publishing

an imprint of Ian Allan Ltd, Terminal House, Station Approach, Shepperton, Surrey TW17 8AS.
Printed by Ian Allan Printing Ltd at its works at Coombelands in Runnymede, England.

Code: 9708/F3

Front cover: **Barnstaple in September 1996, an Atlantic Blue-liveried Mercedes 811D, awaits its driver and passengers at a Red Bus sign!** P. Chancellor

Back cover, top: **A Western National Bristol VR disembarks from the Torpoint ferry on the Torpoint-Plymouth service.** Stewart J. Brown

Back cover, bottom: **Though British Bus had a reputation for not buying many new buses, it bought more in its last years. Particularly impressive were Northern Counties Palatine 2-bodied Volvo Olympians for Northumbria.** Stewart J. Brown

Title page: **For some 25 years Nottingham's double-deckers had bodywork of a distinctive style. The last bodies to a uniquely Nottingham specification were delivered by East Lancs in 1988/89 on 15 Volvo Citybuses and 10 Leyland Lions. This is a Citybus. The two-door body has 85 seats. See page 119.** David Barrow

British Bus

A Rough Ride

Stephen Morris, editor of *Buses*, looks back over the history of one of the major bus groups in Britain

Above:
In the later years of British Bus there was some stocking up on new buses primarily with East Lancs bodywork. If any type could be considered a British bus standard, it is the Dennis Dart with East Lancs EL2000 bodywork, like this Midland Red North one — looking rather incongruous in the 1930s-style Midland Red livery used by this operator until recently — in Wolverhampton.
Stephen Morris

It would be interesting, would it not, had the great, late Lord Ridley not passed away, to know what he thought of the shape of the British bus industry today. Lord, then Nicholas, Ridley, as you no doubt recall, set in motion sweeping changes in the bus industry as Transport Secretary in the mid-1980s, by sweeping away service regulation and public sector ownership. Not wishing to put words in his mouth now he's no longer with us to defend himself (though he made the average rhinoceros seem a sensitive soul by comparison, such was the apparent imperviousness of his hide to his criticism) I'm sure, as a good politician, he would tell us that deregulation and privatisation of the bus industry has been a success. But regardless of the rights and wrongs of what has happened over the last 12 years or so, there are certain aspects of the shape of the British bus industry in the late-1990s that fall short of his ideals and would, no doubt, be a great disappointment to him.

For one thing, he longed for a bus industry of lots of small companies all competing with each other. For another, he longed to bring in expertise from outside the bus industry, with outside interests buying into it and bringing new ways with them. A proposal to break NBC into three conglomerates was dismissed by Lord Ridley as 'cuckoo', yet his beloved market forces, in which he believed so passionately, have created more or less that state of affairs dismissed so disdainfully.

Hindsight is a wonderful thing, and we can all look now at the structure of the British bus industry, sit back in our armchairs, take a swig of our beer and proclaim in superior fashion, 'Of course it was bound to end up like that. Industries *always* form into a few large conglomerates, it's not something unique to buses.' I've heard that said often; though funnily enough I never remember anyone saying it in 1985 or 1986. For then, if the truth be known, none of us really knew how the pieces of the industry which had just felt the full force of

Mr Ridley's sledgehammer would fall back again — we just like to pretend now that we knew it all along.

An outsider...

What, then, of all these outside interests coming into the bus industry? Well, they were a long time coming. Privatisation of National Bus Company got under way on 14 July 1986, when National Holidays was sold to Pleasurama, which already owned the very large coach operator, Smiths-Shearings. Thereafter the next 15 companies were sold to their managements, and it was January 1987 before another company was sold to an outside interest — National Travel East went to ATL, which was a firm already active in the bus and coach industry. Eight engineering companies were sold to a property developer called Robert Beattie, who seemed more interested in the companies' assets than their business. Thus the 37th NBC operator to be sold, Shamrock & Rambler, almost exactly a year after the first NBC sale, was the first bus and coach operator sold to interests beyond the bus and coach industry.

Hardly one of NBC's more significant subsidiaries, Shamrock & Rambler had been Hants & Dorset's coach operations and had latterly started minibuses in a small way in Bournemouth. At the time of its sale ShamRam had 44 coaches and 29 minibuses, and it was sold to a company called Drawlane Ltd, a subsidiary of a Salisbury-based service industry company called

Endless Holdings. Neither its range of activities nor its resources were 'endless', it just happened to be in a street of that name, presumably one built before the Trades Descriptions Act came into force. We described Drawlane in *Buses* September 1987 as having 'wide ranging interests in industrial and commercial cleaning, water treatment and medical supplies and equipment in Britain and the USA'. Its chairman was one Ray McEnhill, who was very much in the contemporary vein of management, for whom numbers with pound signs in front of them were far more important than fleet numbers or route numbers.

Shamrock & Rambler was perhaps a rather inauspicious start, but early the next year Drawlane was to get its hands on some rather more valuable concerns. Later in 1987 it was selected as preferred bidder for three more companies: Southern National, North Devon and London Country (South West), while another newcomer, Allied Bus Services, was selected to buy Lincolnshire, East Midland (which at that stage were to be sold as a combined business) and Midland Red (North). However, there was a suggestion that Allied Bus Services was indeed allied — to Drawlane — and as the Government had set a limit of three companies to any single buyer, in order to prevent the effect of large groups forming, the sales were cancelled.

Once that little glitch was overcome, Drawlane really did begin to expand. Firstly in January 1988 Midland Red North came its way — the mysterious Allied Bus Services was not heard of again and Lincolnshire and East Midland were sold separately after all, to Yorkshire Traction and East Midland's management respectively. Though to Ray McEnhill turnover meant far more than fleetsize, no doubt the fact that Midland Red North ran 248 buses will give more of an indication of the size and relative significance of that operator to our readers. That company was 58th to be privatised, and still, despite Nicholas Ridley's desire to see new blood in the bus industry, Drawlane was the only significant buyer of NBC companies from outside the industry — and in any case local management stayed put in the operators acquired, taking care of day-to-day operations.

Next was London Country (South West), in February 1988. The four London Country companies, having been split up by Nicholas Ridley, were not in huge demand; all ran in areas where the few significant transport corridors were well-served by rail anyway, leaving bus companies to try and identify any remaining passenger flows there may be in an area of comparatively low population density, astronomic car ownership, with attendant problems of congestion, and high costs. All that was going for them was their proximity to the tendered bus service market in London and large freehold sites in areas where land values were going crazy — and these, in most cases, London Country South West included, were sold separately to property

developers — just as well, given the imminent collapse of the property market.

That should have been enough, given the Government edict on three operating companies per buyer. Yet perhaps Shamrock & Rambler was considered not to be a 'proper' NBC company, because of its small size; whatever the reason Drawlane was uniquely allowed a fourth bite of the cherry and won North Western in March. (Though the bids which fell through would have given Drawlane four companies, Southern National and North Devon were effectively sold as a single company anyway.) The four companies gave Drawlane a good geographic spread, and it had become one of a number of embryo bus groups, with 1,050 buses.

However Drawlane was very soon to go into the world of bus manufacture, too, when Trafalgar House subsidiary John Brown decided towards the end of 1987 to sell East Lancashire Coach Builders, which it had owned since 1963, and trailer manufacturer Craven Tasker. The bus and coach building industry was going through a very lean time as the operating industry was concentrating all its resources on restructuring; East Lancs was down to about 10 bodies per month at the time that Drawlane took it over from its previous parent.

...and an insider

Although Ray McEnhill was still chairman of Drawlane, during 1987 a new managing director had been appointed who represented anything but new thinking from outside the industry. He was Geoffrey Hilditch, one of the best-known names in the municipal sector of the bus industry, well-known from his general managership of first Halifax and later Leicester City Transport. Although Mr Hilditch had officially retired he was not

one to be kept out of bus operation for long; during his retirement he had run Cynon Valley Transport, which mysteriously changed from a drab municipal maroon and cream to a much brighter orange, green and cream — not entirely unlike the traditional Halifax scheme.

Thus as Drawlane expanded he found himself back into the big-time of bus company management, and his influence was immediately felt in vehicle policy; having effectively put Dennis on the map as main supplier to Leicester City Transport, Dominators and Falcons suddenly found their way into three of the four Drawlane fleets, all bodied by East Lancs. Dominators would hardly have been appropriate to the fourth Drawlane fleet, Shamrock & Rambler, which in any case was finding the going tough in Bournemouth. The Bournemouth bus operations ceased before the end of 1988, while the company as a whole was sold on to National Express in April 1989, to become Dorset Travel Services — ironically now part of Yellow Buses, Bournemouth with which S&R was once a competitor.

The race for supremacy

No sooner had the privatisation of NBC finished than companies began to change hands and the future shape of the bus industry began to emerge. At the time there were several which one might have expected to grow and become market leaders and it was a fascinating process to watch which developed and which fell by the wayside.

One which could have gone either way, but was quite evidently struggling to keep on top of its operations, was ATL, and in early 1989 it showed which way it was to go; its largest acquisition, Crosville, was sold to Drawlane and Ray McEnhill gave a pledge that Crosville

would regain 'its place as a flagship company in bus transport services'. Which, of course, it never did. However Drawlane was then able to claim it was the largest private group in the bus industry, with 1,600 vehicles and turnover 'in excess of £70 million' — less than a decade later Stagecoach enjoyed a turnover of 20 times that amount!

Despite its size Drawlane still allowed its subsidiaries considerable autonomy. There were hints that a corporate style of bus livery was on the cards though; Leyland Nationals transferred from Midland Red North to Shamrock & Rambler appeared in a predominantly white livery, with green roof and skirt and a thin yellow line separating the skirt from the white. Crosville, coincidentally, had introduced a livery which was remarkably similar in layout on a batch of Metroriders delivered in the last days of ATL, and also adopted something similar. The style of livery had originated with Midland Red North, but of the other companies North Western had a very strong 'designer' livery which was unchanged, while London Country (South West), following delivery of its first Dennis Dominator in a similar colour scheme and also having received some of Shamrock & Rambler's Leyland Nationals in this 'corporate' style, went to another designer, Ray Stenning, and came up with a bright green with darker green relief and a red stripe, and a new name, London & Country. Of all the liveries brought about by Ray Stenning, this was possibly his most successful and quickly gave the rather jaded fleet a fresh new look — and thereafter corporate image for Drawlane was a thing of the past.

Lack of investment

London & Country's jaded image was partly due to a lack of investment in new buses — something which affected most former NBC companies at the time, and while Drawlane did begin to address the problem, notably with Dennises and also some Volvos bodied by East Lancs, it was not enough to stem a fleet age profile which was beginning to become unacceptable. However, London & Country did better than most of Drawlane's companies, requiring new buses for the London Transport contracts it was winning — these improved the age profile, but not for its traditional passengers who, like those of North Western, Crosville and Midland Red North, were left primarily with an unappealing selection of ageing Leyland Nationals and double-deckers of similar vintage. Indeed

Top:
Quite impressive when new, this North Western Falcon looks rather down at heel, running for Bee Line — or just 'Line' if you go by the fleetname on the side.
Stephen Morris

Above:
Rather a sorry-looking Clydeside Iveco minibus at work in Paisley. Behind is an elderly Alexander-bodied Leyland Leopard, while the failed Fleetline across the road is symptomatic of maintenance problems. Stephen Morris

Drawlane soon gained a reputation for insufficient investment in new buses; the group was aiming to maximise profit with minimum investment, which was soon to saddle it with maintenance problems, not to mention image problems.

Meanwhile the brave words uttered over Crosville were hardly bearing fruit. The company had lost its Welsh operations prior to privatisation, and after deregulation industrial action in Liverpool led to its closure there too. Its problems continued under Drawlane, and it decided to split the company up. It straddled the area between Midland Red North and North Western, and so its southernmost operations at Crewe and Etruria were passed over to Midland Red North and Runcorn and Warrington went to North Western.

A changing structure

The next major expansion came on 4 September 1989 when Midland Fox, the largest of the four parts of Midland Red, was acquired. Midland Fox, based on Leicester, probably had the most lucrative part of Midland Red's empire following the loss of the Birmingham operations to West Midlands PTE, and the company had been growing since privatisation by acquiring a number of local operators including Fairtax, Astill & Jordan and the operations in Loughborough of both Leicester CityBus, which traded there as Trippit, and Kinch. The original privatisation of Midland Fox

had been slightly unusual in that as well as being sold to its management, a 25% shareholding went to independent operator Stevensons of Uttoxeter, which had been transformed from a rather run-down independent into a major force in the northeast Midlands by managing director Julian Peddle, who was to become part of the Drawlane team.

Meanwhile Ribble had sold out to Stagecoach, leading to the situation of Drawlane and Stagecoach having a rather ragged collection of operations around Manchester. East Midland had also put an operation into the area, which had also become part of Stagecoach, while Ribble had acquired the Bee Line minibus operations which had been started up by BET subsidiary United Transport in competition with established Manchester operators. To rationalise things, Stagecoach, in return for North Western's Blackburn operations in Ribble-land, sold the East Midland Frontrunner North West and Bee Line operations along with Ribble's Hulme Hall Road depot in Manchester to Drawlane, which combined them with Crosville's Congleton and Macclesfield depots into a new Bee Line Buzz Co under the management of Julian Peddle. By the end of 1989

Soon afterwards it was decided to split London & Country into two parts, effectively splitting off the main London Transport contract operations based at Croydon and Newington Butts, but also including Crawley and Reigate. This was to have greater ramifications in years to come.

those Crosville operations had been separated out into a unit called C-Line, and the rest of Crosville, in its old heartland around Chester, was formed into an autonomous unit under another of Drawlane's 'big guns', Dawson Williams, who had come back into the industry after involvement in Stagecoach as managing director of Hampshire Bus. However Crosville was not to make the grade and was sold out of the group to PMT in February 1990.

Another subsidiary was also formed before the end of 1989, again by internal reorganisation; London & Country had a unit called Speedlink Airport Services which had been formed out of its Heathrow-Gatwick express services, and this was separated out into a new company, which enabled it to develop into new airport-related fields.

London & Country was to gain another subsidiary before the end of 1990, when the neighbouring part of Alder Valley came on to the market. Alder Valley and Berks Bucks had both come into the ownership of Q-Drive, and one of the partners in that company, Dave Stewart, had decided to cash in his shareholding. Rather than saddle the group with debt the other directors decided to sell part of the business to fund the purchase of Mr Stewart's shares, so the Alder Valley operations from Woking, Guildford and Cranleigh were sold, to become London & Country's Guildford & West Surrey subsidiary. Strangely, Midland Fox, continuing its acquisitive nature, had also bought a subsidiary in London & Country's area, Tellings Golden Miller.

New vehicles and new bodies

By this stage Drawlane was running some 2,000 buses. It put some investment in place in new vehicles, though in 1990 and 1991 it bought a total of 159 new buses, of which 36 were Volvo double-deckers required for London Transport work by London & Country and 53 were minibuses, including a much-needed injection of 35 Mercedes-Benz 811Ds into Bee Line, which had finished up with a motley fleet of cast-offs from within the Drawlane group to add to its own Sherpa and Dodge minibuses, both of which were getting on in years for types which did not age graciously. This was scarcely enough to sustain the fleet age profile at its existing level, let alone address the issue of improving it. However, the Group did start looking to East Lancs to bring some improvement, by rebodying Leyland Tiger coaches as service buses for Midland Red North and to develop some means of rejuvenating the vast fleet of ageing Leyland Nationals. Indeed, such was the overall state of the new bus market that refurbishing and rebodying was vital to East Lancs for survival.

It seemed that Drawlane was beginning to reach the end of its expansion; no further acquisitions had been made in 1990 or 1991, though the group was about to enter a new phase.

National Express and British Bus

This was evident when Drawlane led a group comprising mainly finance houses to acquire National Express

Above:
The Greenway project did rather more to the Leyland National than was really necessary, and a cheaper option developed later was the Urban Bus, keeping more of the original body and using a Cummins B-series/Allison driveline similar to a Dennis Dart. London & Country SNC420 was one of the first; unusually this was a 10.3m vehicle, and real Dennis Darts were considered a better bet for vehicles this size. The intention was to refurbish 11.3m Nationals in this way, but a change of engineering director brought a new regime of new buses instead. Stephen Morris

Group. In addition to its nationwide coach operations National Express included Crosville Wales, Amberline, Carlton PSV and coach-operating subsidiaries, and it was sold for £10.25 million, seemingly a large amount at the time though soon to seem like peanuts as prices for bus companies began to soar. Drawlane's shareholding in National Express was 25%, and chairman Ray McEnhill became chairman and chief executive of National Express.

Much emphasis was laid on the fact that this was not a merger and that National Express was not to be considered a part of the Drawlane group. Indeed, in due course it became apparent that National Express was to seek listing on the London Stock Exchange, and to that end began to rationalise its activities. Crosville Wales' National Express diagrams passed to its Amberline subsidiary and National Express announced that Crosville Wales would be placed on the market; indeed Oswestry garage passed quickly to Midland Red North. At the same time Speedlink Airport Services, with its coaching pedigree, was passed over from Drawlane to National Express.

The flotation of National Express was achieved by December 1992, and that group has gone on to expand into airports, motorway service stations, railway franchises and urban bus operation on a major scale, not least with Travel West Midlands. In anticipation a new company called Surecapital PLC was established in October 1992 to take over the operations of Drawlane, which it did from 1 November, and when the flotation of National Express was completed on 10 December Surecapital PLC was renamed British Bus PLC. It retained the Endless Street head office in Salisbury. The long-term intention was that British Bus would also float, and it too started to rationalise its activities.

Ray McEnhill was now chairman of National Express and chief executive Adam Mills also moved over to the same job at National Express; thus Dawson Williams became British Bus's chief executive, and National Express went its own way, entirely independently of the new group. However, Crosville Wales came to British Bus in its entirety. Meanwhile, in its bid to concentrate on bus operations, British Bus quickly sold East Lancs to its management, though Dawson Williams led the management buyout and subsequently became East Lancs' outright owner.

Thus East Lancs continued as a major supplier to British Bus — when British Bus bought any buses, that was. However East Lancs and London & Country together had developed the Greenway refurbishment of Leyland Nationals, which reprocessed the vehicles into what were effectively new buses, though at about half the price and not requiring to meet the latest legislation on emissions etc. This enabled East Lancs to be able to offer either new or rebuilt Gardner 6LHXB engines in Greenways after the type was no longer available in new buses, and few British Bus subsidiaries did not get at least a handful of Greenways. In the case of London & Country, which still had not got round to addressing the issue of replacing its very elderly fleet of buses, outside its London Transport contract work, the Greenway was to form a substantial part of the full-size single-deck fleet. Meanwhile Midland Red North amassed a fleet of 27 of its East Lancs-rebodied Leyland Tigers.

Dawson Williams pledged continued expansion of the group which would 'seize every opportunity to acquire businesses that will provide sound growth for the Group in the UK, in Europe and worldwide'. There was a promise of fleet replacement being a priority and development of interests in rail privatisation and guided busways.

That may have been the intention, though still British Bus lagged behind the other groups in terms of fleet replacement. Indeed, in its first full year it bought only 14 large buses, and that after three years of famine in that direction. All were East Lancs-bodied Dennises, including five Darts, three for North Western and two for London & Country. There were also a few minibuses.

Interest there may have been in rail privatisation and guided busways, but the group was not to figure in the rail privatisation process at all and still has no involvement in guided buses. However, there was some growth overseas, with a consultancy operation busy in Warsaw. Three lefthand-drive Dennis Lances had MetSec bodies assembled by East Lancs for use there.

More smaller acquisitions

Some of British Bus's companies continued to buy subsidiaries of their own; perhaps the strangest were Stanbridge & Crichel and Oakfield Travel, both in Dorset, which became rather remote subsidiaries of Guildford & West Surrey, itself a subsidiary of London & Country, a subsidiary of British Bus!

British Bus's next major acquisition also became a subsidiary of London & Country; this was its first foray into the former municipal sector, when it acquired Southend Transport during 1993. The acquisition of Scottish Citylink by National Express brought two small operators British Bus's way, Bruce of Airdrie, which had been owned by Citylink, and Express Travel, Perth, owned by National Express, and Bruce was closed down almost immediately. British Bus had also relieved National Express of Amberline, its bus operations

becoming a subsidiary of North Western. Together Amberline and Express Travel ran some 80 coaches, nearly all contracted to National Express.

Under British Bus's policy of allowing its subsidiaries to take over smaller companies, North Western expanded again during 1993 by taking over one of the three major independents which had started up in Merseyside since deregulation. Fareway passed to Merseybus in the April of that year, and North Western acquired Liverline, with 51 buses, a couple of months later. From the end of August North Western also took on responsibility for Bee Line, and C-Line had been reorganised out of existence, split between Bee Line and Midland Red North.

Meanwhile the unlikely combination of a Surrey operator owned by a Leicestershire firm owned by a Salisbury-based group running in Cardiff came about, when Tellings Golden Miller, the Midland Fox subsidiary, set up in opposition to Cardiff Bus with an operation which came to be called Cardiff Bluebird, though TGM was soon sold back to its previous owner, Steve Telling. More divestment of smaller operators came with the sale of Stanbridge & Crichel and Oakfield Travel to Damory Coaches less than a year after their acquisition.

British Bus ended 1993 by acquiring the other Essex municipality, Colchester, in November. Colchester Borough Transport was losing money following an onslaught of competition from Badgerline subsidiary

Eastern National, and like Southend became a subsidiary of London & Country. It gave two British Bus outposts in Badgerline territory. Colchester, despite its recent financial instability, had invested in a modern fleet of Leyland Olympians and Lynxes, which were useful for dispersing around the Group to lower the age profile of fleets such as Crosville Wales — which was renamed Crosville Cymru — in return for older Leyland National 2s spoiling the good age profile at Colchester.

By the end of 1993 British Bus had a combined fleet of around 2,400 vehicles and its annual turnover had increased to £100 million. The main fleets in its ownership were Amberline, Bee Line, Colchester Borough Transport, Crosville Cymru, Express Travel, Guildford & West Surrey, Liverline, London & Country, Midland Fox, Midland Red North and North Western, in addition to numerous smaller companies which were subsidiaries of some of these. It also owned a percentage

Right:
Within British Bus London & Country and East Lancs developed the National Greenway as a way of recycling the hundreds of old Leyland Nationals in the group. The very first was this ex-North Western National 2 which has spent its working life as a Greenway at Addlestone garage of London & Country — and still brings the writer to work some days. Later ones have a rather more stylish front.
Stephen Morris

Below:
Perhaps the most unusual new buses have been London & Country's East Lancs-bodied Dennis Arrows.
Stephen Morris

of Rhondda, which had been set up following the demise of National Welsh in 1992. It was the third biggest bus group in Britain, though it lagged well behind the largest two — Stagecoach and Badgerline — both of which by now were, like National Express, quoted on the London Stock Exchange, giving them access to plentiful funds for acquisition, expansion and asset renewal. If British Bus were to stay in the big league it needed to do something similar.

Above:
Another unusual British Bus type was the Scania L113 with the East Lancs FlexCi body, a rather square style derived from the MaxCi low-floor bus but executed rather more neatly. Gade Valley is part of The Shires, which may sound like a pub but is in fact Luton & District. The 'SE' prefix to its fleetnumber shows that Gade Valley is part of what was London & Country (North West), where such prefixes are in keeping with the London Transport origins of this part of the company. M. E. Lyons

A missed opportunity

It appeared that British Bus was poised for expansion again at the end of 1993, when it was named as preferred bidder for GM Buses North, the sale of which was being driven by the Government. Though due to be completed by the end of the year the sale was delayed as there were monopoly implications; British Bus was already very active in Merseyside and Greater Manchester and the acquisition of GMBN would give it dominance in the region. However, the Office of Fair Trading cleared the sale without it being referred to the Monopolies & Mergers Commission, and the Government gave a new deadline of 31 March 1994 for the sale to be completed.

However, just before the sale was completed the shareholders committee of Greater Manchester PTA, which was selling the business, suddenly decided to sell the business to its employees instead. The Secretary of State for Transport rejected the employees bid, and three days before the deadline for completion new bids were invited from British Bus and the employee team. In the

event the latter won, and officially the sale was completed at two minutes to midnight on the deadline date, 31 March — though an insider tells me the clock stopped for an hour or two!

Springboard to the big time

British Bus was still pursuing its aim of achieving a Stock Exchange flotation, but was not yet ready. However it took an important step forward in the spring of 1994 by selling 40% of its shares to an investment group and taking out a loan of £30 million from the Bank of Boston. This was a time when Badgerline and Stagecoach were expanding rapidly, and there was the danger of suitable bus companies to acquire being snapped up, leaving British Bus where it was and becoming more and more of an also-ran.

Altogether this move gave British Bus access to £65 million for capital development — and subsequently the Bank of Boston loan facility was increased to £110 million — and the group restructured again.

Above:
Midland Fox has an Urban Fox offshoot in Leicester. British Bus's last order for new buses — its biggest ever — included some Northern Counties-bodied Volvo Olympians. Tim Carter

Amberline and Express Travel were sold to the group of former managers which owned East Lancs at the beginning of the year; these two companies were loss-making and their disposal gave the group a healthier profile for its new investors. They were later sold to their own management, and, given the history of British Bus and National Express, the unthinkable happened in that Express Travel set up its own express network in competition with National Express. Like other similar attempts it was not to endure.

Meanwhile, British Bus set up another new company, British Bus Group Ltd, which took over British Bus PLC from 5 May 1994. The first acquisition was Stevensons of Uttoxeter.

Though on the surface a small family-owned business, Stevensons had expanded vigorously over the previous 10 years, not least with its takeover of East Staffordshire, and ran 300 buses from 10 garages. It was under pressure, however, as a foray into West Midlands' territory had brought a response from that operator in Stevenson's heartland in Burton. British Bus also acquired the 49% share in Stevensons which East Staffordshire District Council had taken as part of the deal giving Stevensons control of the buses in Burton. It was also usefully placed for British Bus, fitting in nicely between Midland Fox and Midland Red North. Under British Bus Stevensons was to expand further, taking over the former C-Line operations in North Cheshire from Midland Red North.

The takeover of Stevensons was concluded in June 1994, and was followed immediately by the takeover of

Luton & District, which also included London Country (North West). In its early days Luton & District also helped out other companies looking to achieve management buyouts. Lincoln City Transport had not been one of the more successful, and was sold on to its neighbour, Road Car, but Luton & District still had sizeable interests in Derby City Transport and Clydeside 2000, both of which decided to sell the rest of their shares to British Bus, giving the group a third former municipality and its first sizeable presence in bus operation in Scotland — though with it were to come some major headaches, as Clydeside 2000 was operating in the hotly-contested areas of Renfrewshire, one of the few areas of the country where competition was so intense that in some instances the basic rules of the game had been thrown out of the window. Clydeside's ageing fleet was causing apoplexy to the local vehicle inspectorate and when British Bus did finally get round to a serious programme of vehicle replacement resources had to be ploughed into Clydeside 2000 in order to safeguard its operating licence.

Next came the Proudmutual Group, which included Northumbria and Kentish Bus & Coach. Having gone some way to recreating the old Midland Red, British Bus

14

Above:
While new buses are the order of the day, older refurbished buses have continued to enter service, not least with North Western, which had a number of Metrobuses and Leyland Nationals from West Midlands. This Leyland National is used on Bee Line services in Manchester. John Mushet

was now managing to rebuild the former London Country; it already owned what had been London Country (South West), with Luton & District had come London Country (North West) and also some of the Stevenage operations which Luton & District had acquired from Sovereign, and one of the constituents of London Country (North East) and Kentish Bus was what had been London Country (South East).

Within seven months British Bus had doubled its turnover to £200 million and increased its fleet size to 3,700; it was now snapping at the heels of Badgerline for No 2 slot in the bus group league tables. However the ground was permanently shifting around this time, as management buyout companies from the early days of privatisation of both National Bus Company and Scottish Bus Group decided the time was right to cash in their investments, and Stagecoach and Badgerline were also taking great expansionist steps. By and large the smaller groups were now out of the running for expansion, even though the privatisation of London Buses gave some opportunities. While Stagecoach gained two London companies, the other main beneficiaries were Go-Ahead, which acquired London Central and then went on to buy London General from its management, and the Cowie Group.

The Cowie Group

Cowie was not a big player in buses, though as a company was quite substantial, being involved largely with vehicle dealing, leasing and finance. It had acquired the Ewer Group in 1980, which brought with its portfolio of motor dealers a London-based coach firm, Grey-Green, and as no-one else wanted to buy it off them Cowie decided to keep it going. As is well-known Grey-Green was the shining example of an independent operator doing all the right things in the London bus tendering market, and during the late-1980s the emphasis shifted away from coaches towards London buses.

There had been a strong possibility of expansion in the bus and coach manufacturing market, when Cowie had tried to buy up one of its main rivals in the car dealing world, Henlys, which would have brought Plaxton with it, but this was not to be. However it acquired Leaside in the London bus privatisation process and was persuaded to take South London too. South London was a rather sad business at the time; with rather bad timing it had fallen foul of the licensing authorities over poor maintenance, just as privatisation was in full swing, and having its licence curtailed wiped millions off its value. Cowie was persuaded that the engineering expertise

within Leaside could sort out South London, which indeed it did, and Cowie was all of a sudden big in buses.

Up to No 2

Surprisingly neither British Bus nor FirstBus, formed out of the amalgamation of Badgerline and GRT Holdings, had any success in London privatisation, though both had tendered operations through existing subsidiaries. Indeed during 1994 British Bus reorganised London & Country and Kentish Bus, joining forces in the middle to create Londonlinks, engaged primarily in London bus operations.

However just prior to the combining of Badgerline and GRT to form FirstBus British Bus managed to climb up to No 2 in the league tables by acquiring Caldaire Holdings in March 1995. This brought West Riding, Yorkshire Woollen, Selby & District and South Yorkshire Road Transport and around 400 buses. Then on 18 April Maidstone & District joined the fold. There had been speculation for some time that M&D, one of the last remaining independent former NBC operators, would sell either to FirstBus or Stagecoach, and M&D

put out a statement denying that the firm was for sale towards the end of 1994. None the less the sale to British Bus was completed in April 1995, and M&D was later placed into a new sub-group called Invictaway, based in Maidstone and also incorporating Kentish Bus and Londonlinks. This was to be the last major acquisition by British Bus, which now had a combined fleet of more than 5,000, 11,000 staff and a turnover of £280 million a year.

New buses at last

British Bus at last accepted that it couldn't go on with a fleet which was for ever getting older. Its recent acquisitions had lowered the overall age profile, as all had kept up a policy of fleet renewal in independent

Above:
Much of Crosville Cymru's operation requires minibuses; for a long time it fared rather better than other British Bus companies in being able to obtain new ones, such as this Alexander-bodied Mercedes-Benz 709D, seen at Rhyl in its first week of service in August 1995. R. L. Wilson

hands; the Yorkshire operators in particular had a very impressive fleet of Leyland Lynxes, Volvo B10Bs, Dennis Lances and Optare MetroRiders which contrasted with tatty Leyland Nationals, Leyland Atlanteans and Bristol VRs elsewhere in the group. The combination of old buses and high fares which characterised much of British Bus's operation may be a good recipe for high profits, but is not one for long-term growth. With higher standards being imposed on the industry in general, maintenance costs of old buses were beginning to swing the equation in favour of new buses, especially where vehicles such as the Dennis Dart meant that these were available at lower cost than had been the case in recent years anyway.

Thus during 1994 new buses began to arrive in some quantity; not enough to stem the tide of the ageing fleet, but it was a start. There were 40 new double-deckers, 20 Scanias for Midland Fox and 20 Volvo Olympians for London & Country, all with East Lancs bodywork, while Derby, Midland Red North, London & Country and North Western shared 43 Dennis Darts, most of them bodied by East Lancs. Volvo B6s went to Clydeside (seven) and London & Country (five) while 90 Mercedes minibuses also went in, and there were four new low-floor Dennis Lances for Southend.

Meanwhile the new acquisitions were bringing in new buses; during 1994 the Proudmutual companies had 77 new vehicles, many of them Northern Counties-bodied Volvo B6s for Kentish Bus, a type also going into Luton

& District, which had taken 32, though British Bus cancelled the residue of the order before all were delivered. Another 20 had been expected. There were also used buses, in the shape of Metrobuses and Leyland Nationals from West Midlands Travel, which were refurbished and put into service replacing older-generation vehicles in the Bee Line fleet of North Western.

Following the acquisition of Maidstone & District its engineering director, David Powell, was promoted to engineering director for the group, and it was he who decided that new buses were needed. He put an end to the programme of refurbishing older buses, effectively killing the Greenway project and also a promising lower-cost alternative being developed by Northumbria and London & Country, incorporating a Dennis Dart driveline into a refurbished Leyland National structure. Thus for 1995 a new vehicle programme involving 344 buses was announced. Priority was to get some new buses into Clydeside, which took 10 Plaxton-bodied Dennis Lances — a further 10 went to North Western. Much of the order was to be bodied by East Lancs, and

included the first 10 Dennis Arrows and 15 Lances for London & Country, while 100 Scanias were also ordered, many with a new design of East Lancs body on the L113 chassis.

There were other odd batches of buses during the year too; the renewing of the Clydeside fleet brought a variety of vehicles from dealer stock, there were low-floor Lances for London & Country and low-floor Scanias for Starline, a company taken over by North Western during the year, and Kentish Bus, all with Wrights bodywork. Northumbria had 13 Scanias with East Lancs' new Cityzen double-deck body and Crosville Wales took four MAN/Optare Vectas. Volvo at this time was very much out of favour, and London & Country's requirement for four low-height double-deckers was met by four Dennis Dominators, the first built since the end of 1992 and the last to be built at all. They arrived in March 1996.

More was to come, with orders for around 500 new buses announced for 1996, including 224 low-floor Dennis Darts, 97 of them to be bodied by East Lancs with its new Spryte body, the rest by Plaxton, 73 more East Lancs-bodied Scanias and, following the healing of the rift with Volvo, 65 Olympians with Northern Counties bodies. Interestingly the proportion of new minibuses was reduced, with 126 Mercedes and 45 Optare MetroRiders. By September 1996 58% of the fleet was under 10 years old, 29% under five years old, and the average fleet age was 9.2 years, though there were still more than 2,000 buses in the fleet over 10 years old, 1,300 of them over 15 years old.

Troubled times and a sell-out

Meanwhile British Bus had stumbled into trouble. Whilst preparing at last for its great ambition to float the company in July 1995 accusations raised their heads over alleged irregularities involving the Bank of Boston loan and two of British Bus's directors, including Dawson Williams. Whatever the substance of these allegations, flotation was out of the question while enquiries were continuing and there was widespread doubt as to the future of British Bus. Typical bus industry rumours sprang up that the group was about to go bankrupt (far from it, it always returned a healthy profit), that it would sell off its subsidiaries piecemeal… for once though there was little suggestion that Stagecoach or FirstBus would buy it, given the monopoly implications.

However a buyer did emerge, in the shape of the Cowie Group. Cowie had decided it would continue to expand in buses, and had already relieved West Midlands Travel of its County Bus & Coach subsidiary. Its offer, made on 18 June 1996, included conditions that the Serious Fraud Office investigations should not rebound on it and that there would be no announcement of a Monopolies & Mergers Commission investigation.The latter seemed highly likely to come about; Cowie's interests in South London abutted those of Londonlinks, Kentish Bus and London & Country while those in North London came close to The Shires, as Luton & District had been retitled. Moreover County Bus fitted another piece of the old London Country jigsaw into British Bus's portfolio.

None the less the deal was completed, in August, and the next day Cowie announced it was to relieve West Midlands Travel of yet more of its subsidiaries, in this case North East Bus, whose United and Tees & District operations abutted British Bus's Northumbria operation. Indeed Northumbria had been created solely because United was considered too big to privatise in its old form.

Not surprisingly, the MMC did investigate; more surprisingly it gave the new group a clean bill of health and did not require it to take any action.

So far the Cowie Group has not declared its hand as to its further direction. No doubt the much-needed fleet renewal will continue, though what buses will be involved remains to be seen. As part of its motor dealing activities Cowie owns Hughes-DAF, the DAF importer into Britain, and has already appointed it to look after vehicle acquisition for the bus group. Whether this will mean a huge influx of DAFs remains to be seen, though it seems unlikely that DAF Bus, at its present scale, would be able to fulfil all of Cowie's needs. Hughes-DAF is already a dealer for the Dennis Dart, so no doubt Darts will continue to flow in. As for bodywork, Cowie cancelled the outstanding British Bus orders at East Lancs, transferring most of them to Plaxton — perhaps a surprising move, given that Plaxton and Northern Counties are part of the rival Henlys group.

Of the three main groups British Bus has certainly been the most inauspicious. Though catching up now, its bus fleet has looked old and tatty alongside Stagecoach and FirstBus. Its lack of corporate identity has enabled local bus companies to get on and do their own thing, and has brought less attention from the Monopolies & Mergers Commission than has been experienced by the groups which make more of a 'thing' of corporate identity, but there have been numerous corporate restructures which cannot have made life too stable. So much for the one group which apparently introduced outside interests to the British bus industry.

British Bus Group Ltd main subsidiaries, 1995

Bee Line Buzz
Clydeside 2000
Colchester Borough Transport
Crosville Cymru
Derby City Transport
Express Travel
Hunters of Seaton Delaval
Kentish Bus & Coach
London & Country
Luton & District
Maidstone & District
Midland Fox
Midland Red North
North Western
Northumbria Motor Services
Selby & District
Southend Transport
South Yorkshire Road Transport
Stevensons of Uttoxeter
West Riding
Yorkshire Woollen District

Nottingham Lions

Roy Marshall looks back.

The later version of the Leyland Lion — the LT5A, LT7 and LT8 models — played an important part in and around Nottingham in the early days of my interest in buses. This was not surprising considering that over 130 of them entered service locally, although after the LT5A, the major combine group companies had preferred the more powerful six-cylinder Tiger, usually with an oil engine.

Barton Transport, however, had been forced by the new Construction and Use Regulations (introduced under the 1930 Road Traffic Act) to replace most of their in-house constructed or modified chassis, mainly based on Lancias, with more mundane vehicles. From 1932 their choice was the LT5 Lion. They continued to specify the petrol-engined Lion until 1939, underlining the fact that although they were a publicly-quoted company they were still independently-minded. Skills, a Nottingham-based operator, had one Lion which was oil-engined but which after a few years was fitted with a petrol unit.

As elsewhere, the purchase of a certain model by an important operator rubbed off on smaller independents. In the case of the Lion in Nottingham this was helped by

Above:
G. V. Dennis, trading as Robin Hood Transport, bought only one Lion, a Brush-bodied LT5A in 1934. It was quickly sold, with the more powerful Tiger model proving more suitable for the company's Blackpool express service. It eventually ended up in the Barton fleet. Brush

Below:
An unusual Lion rebuild by Barton involved lengthening the chassis and also stretching a 1948 Duple body from 27ft 6in to 30ft to produce a long Lion. A diesel engine provided added power. The body came from a PS1/1 Tiger which was being rebuilt for further service with a new body. Roy Marshall

a local Leyland agency. For 20 years from their introduction, my trips to visit various relatives, together with journeys to Leicester, Loughborough, Melton Mowbray and Derby were by Lion. Each year the latest Barton intake would be put on the Nottingham to Derby service until the Titan TD7s arrived.

The four-cylinder engine in the Lion produced a melodic tick-tick which together with the hiss from the carburettor was quite pleasant. On hills such as Derby Road, Nottingham, they may have been slow compared to current vehicles but they never appeared to be under strain. Downhill they would sometimes backfire but this was fairly commonplace on petrol-engined commercial vehicles in those days. A great explosion could be created by quickly switching the ignition off and on as a Skill's driver reported gleefully one day. He had tried this trick out on an office girl collecting a tray of food and drink from a local café. She dropped the lot!

These were the days of 12V starting systems, making cold starting difficult on a winter's day. This had to be overcome by the use of the starting handle by one man, or by two using a rope. A sudden, sharp, reverse on the

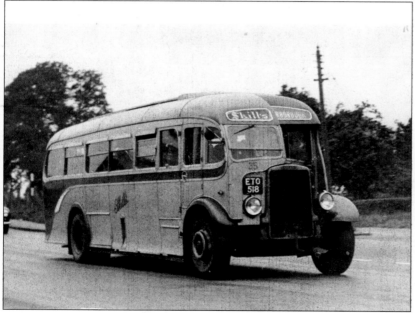

handle could produce broken teeth, dentures or wrists, but the unfortunate recipient of such injuries would never have dreamed of claiming damages as would be the case today.

In later years both Barton and Skills rebodied their Lions with bodies removed from early postwar chassis which were needed for conversions and rebodying. In such instances the larger oil engines replaced the original petrol units thus ensuring that Lions remained in service until the mid-1950s, shortly before I left the city.

Top:
Two of Barton's 1934 Lions had 39-seat Willowbrook bus bodies — a high capacity for the day. They were rebodied by Duple in 1939 at the start of a policy of having a 10-year chassis life and a five-year body life. G. H. F. Atkins

Above:
Squires of Ruddington ran this Brush-bodied LT5A on its service into Nottingham. It passed into Barton ownership in 1935. Brush

Top and above:
In October 1953 this 1936 Lion had been withdrawn. In most fleets that would have meant a final trip to the scrapyard, but with Barton's interest in rebodying and rebuilding, the ageing Lion was fitted with the Duple body, 7.4-litre engine and chromed radiator from a 1948 PS1/1 Tiger. Roy Marshall

HIGHLAND HOLIDAY

In 1975 a youthful **Mark Bailey** went to Scotland on a family holiday, with Skye as the destination. Here's some of what he saw.

Right:
Looking at first glance like a Bedford SB, this 1959 Duple Vega body hides a 1949 Maudslay Marathon III chassis. New to MacBrayne, in 1975 it was owned by MacTavish of Arrochar, whose depot was on the banks of Loch Lomond.
ALL PHOTOGRAPHS BY THE AUTHOR

Below:
Taylor of Badcaul, trading as Westerbus, connected Inverness with Laide using this spartan Bedford VAS1 with Marshall body. It had been new to Coventry Corporation.

Left:
Among Highland Omnibuses' second-hand acquisitions were some ex-Edinburgh Titans with forward-entrance Alexander bodies. These included this PD3/2 with unique Homalloy front. Behind it stands a hired Western SMT Albion Lowlander

Below:
Alexander-bodied Bedfords were rare. Highland Omnibuses had six VAM5s with Y-type bodies which were unusual in lacking the distinctive roof-mounted destination display which was a feature of most Y-types. These were coaches, in Highland's blue and grey livery.

Above:
Highland Omnibuses built up a large fleet of Fords. Most were bought new, but second-hand examples included this Strachan-bodied R226 which had been new to Evan Evans of London. Highland's bus livery was poppy red and peacock blue — two colours which come out looking remarkably similar on black and white film.

Left:
Seen en route to the north, the last AEC Regent supplied new to a Scottish operator. Owned by Garelochhead Coach Services, it had bodywork by Northern Counties. The location is Helensburgh, where it was operating the town service.

Left
Alexander (Northern) ran into Inverness, generally using AEC Reliances. Although over 15 years old, this Alexander-bodied machine looked remarkably smart.

Below:
MacBrayne's coach tours were taken over by Alexander (Midland) in 1970 and along with them came a fleet of Duple-bodied Bedford VAS5s. One pauses in Inverness. Alexander (Midland) coach drivers still wore lightweight tunics in the summer, and had white tops on their hats — this driver's hat is sitting in the offside corner of the windscreen.

Above:
Vehicle shortages were a recurring feature of Highland Omnibuses' operations, and second-hand or hired buses were frequently drafted in from other Scottish Bus Group companies. In 1975 Western SMT provided this 1961 Bristol MW6G with a 41-seat Alexander body. It is seen at Inverness bus station.

Right:
Among the smaller operators on Skye was Sutherland of Glenbrittle, running from Carbost to Portree where this ex-Highland AEC Reliance was photographed. It had Park Royal bodywork.

Top:
On the Isle of Skye, Highland Omnibuses had succeeded MacBrayne as the major operator. This ex-MacBrayne Reliance had a Willowbrook body and was laying over in Portree after working the service from Glasgow to Uig, which provided onward connections by ferry to the Western Isles.

Above:
The ferry from Uig ran to Tarbert on Harris, where Highland Omnibuses briefly ran the former MacBrayne services. Among the vehicles on Harris was this Bedford SB1 with Burlingham body. Highland withdrew from Harris in 1976, its vehicles and operations being taken over by Harris Garage.

Top:
Despite the destination display, this Bedford SB5 of Hebridean Transport was running the service from Tarbert to Stornoway. Note the bus seats and deep sliding windows in the Duple Dominant coach body.

Above:
Typical of buses serving Stornoway is this Bedford SB8 with Duple Midland body, seen in the town's bus stance. It was operated by Hebridean Transport.

Brief Revivals

The privatisation of the National Bus Company in the 1980s prompted several of its former subsidiaries to revive the liveries they had abandoned more than 12 years before. **Peter Rowlands** looks back at their efforts, and traces what came of them.

Above:
NBC made red and white look unappealing. Northern showed what could be done by adopting this layout and a deeper shade of red. The bus is one of the unusual Willowbrook-bodied VRTs bought by NBC for Northern and East Kent.
ALL PHOTOGRAPHS BY THE AUTHOR

Above:
The Midland Red retro livery adopted by Midland Red North suffered from being somewhat drab. A Leyland Tiger with Belfast-built Alexander bodywork illustrates the effect.

Can you revive a long-discontinued bus livery and get away with it? And in particular, can you do it if the livery is strongly traditional, and has unmistakable overtones of an earlier era?

It's one of those ideas that come up periodically as bus operators look for new ways to present themselves to the world. On the whole, it's fairly rare to find the concept actually carried through. Often a bus company will paint one or two of its buses in a former livery to celebrate some anniversary, but that doesn't really count; the revival can only be regarded as wholehearted if the entire fleet takes on the retrospective style.

There have been isolated instances of this over the years. In the early 1980s, for instance, Blackburn Transport dropped its 1970s look — a rather unsubtle red, white and dark green — and reverted to an earlier and more sober mid-green. And a version of the erstwhile Halifax Corporation cream and green livery resurfaced at Aberdare, South Wales, for the local authority operations of Cynon Valley when Halifax's one-time General Manager, Geoff Hilditch, took control there.

However, the most wide-ranging and prolonged move to reinvent old liveries probably came later in the 1980s when the National Bus Company was broken up and privatised. To understand the circumstances you have to glance back at its history.

In 1971, the Government-owned NBC was running most of the big bus fleets of England and Wales that were not under local authority control. But although created by the merger of the BET and Tilling bus groups three years earlier, it had no unifying identity. Few of its customers had even heard of it.

To remedy this perceived deficiency it abandoned dozens of the familiar liveries of its constituent companies, and adopted instead a uniform all-over poppy red or leaf green. The face of the British bus industry was changed for ever.

It was 12 long years before the relentless grip of those two colour schemes was loosened — by which time the prospect of a deregulated and privatised bus industry was looming. Freed from the compulsion to toe the corporate line, NBC's member companies were then able to reassert their presence on the local scene, and the industry watched with fascination to see how they would do it.

In practice, change came in a piecemeal fashion, starting even before privatisation began in 1986. Subsidiaries such as the Go-Ahead Group and neighbouring United were quite tentative at first, sticking to the existing red but adding more white relief and brighter fleetnames. Others were immediately ambitious; Bristol Omnibus, in particular, launched an extraordinary new red, yellow and blue colour scheme in April 1985, and to this day it remains a benchmark for adventurous bus liveries.

What many industry-watchers wondered was which companies (if any) would revert to their pre-NBC liveries. Although the passing of these schemes

Left:
West Yorkshire was taken over by Yorkshire Rider. A VRT in Tilling red carries its new owner's fleetname.

Below left:
Alder Valley's final livery looked back to the great days of Aldershot & District, but in a modern style. A Leyland National hurries through Basingstoke.

Right:
The modern face of Stagecoach South, with corporate livery on a Hampshire Bus VRT. This has displaced a variety of liveries along the south coast, including East Kent, Southdown and Hampshire Bus.

Below:
Gold-underlined fleetnames in a quasi-Tilling style on a Tilling red VRT operated by West Yorkshire in Harrogate in 1988.

had been much lamented, the industry was now 12 years
further down the road. Could the old liveries hold their
own in a changed and more competitive environment, or
would they be regarded merely as diversions into the
realms of nostalgia?

The first hint of a revival turned out to be a false trail.
Following the division of Midland Red into four
companies, as early as 1982 the new Midland Red East
company started to paint its vehicles in a deep all-over
red similar to the pre-NBC hue. It was one of the very
first signs that NBC red was no longer sacrosanct. But
would pukka 'Midland' fleetnames follow?

By no means. This turned out to be a prelude to the
launch of the new Midland Fox identity. In 1983 a rather
brash yellow stripe was added to the new red scheme,
and later the Fox emblem was introduced. As it turned
out, the former Midland Red image did eventually make

a reappearance, but that would not be until a remarkable
10 years later. For the time being, Midland Red
remained no more than a name.

It was in the Yorkshire area where pre-NBC liveries
made their first strong reappearance, and one of the first
companies to go this way was Yorkshire Traction. Its
gesture of defiance at the NBC image was in fact a fairly
plain new dark red livery, launched in 1986, but this did
have a traditional-style underlined fleetname. The aim
was evidently to achieve an effect rather than to imitate
the past too fastidiously. In the reputed heartland of the
bus operating world, the company perhaps felt little need
to prove anything to the purists; but a nod at tradition
helped assert the company's independence.

The main company's new image was supplemented by
others; for instance, the old Mexborough & Swinton
identity made a reappearance. A little further west,
another old name, County Motors, was revived by a
fellow company, West Riding, in a somewhat similar
spirit.

Yet just as these traditional-style identities had slipped
in without great fanfare, so they eventually slipped out
again as the companies moved on. There was no wailing
or gnashing of teeth; as the 1990s unfolded, the
operators simply upgraded their image to something
more in keeping with the times.

Up in the Leeds area, there had been a rather more
dramatic development. Here, in the late 1980s, West
Yorkshire Road Car did what enthusiasts everywhere
had probably hoped secretly that one of the ex-NBC
companies would do: it revived the old Tilling red livery.

Above left:
**Stagecoach has added a touch of class to its East London
Routemasters with gold fleetnames and fleetnumbers and a dark
cream relief band. Other new owners of former London Buses
subsidiaries have not been quite as imaginative.**

Left:
County revived, on an ECW-bodied Olympian.

Above:
**Midland Fox was one of the first NBC companies to adopt a
radically new livery with its distinctive yellow and red. This is an
ECW-bodied Olympian.**

This was the colour scheme that had been worn by half the buses in the Tilling fleets, nationalised after the war and later combined with the BET fleets to form NBC. It started to creep in during 1986, then the revival gradually gathered pace.

In a field beset with paradoxes, this was undoubtedly one. Tilling red had itself represented a kind of uniformity in its day, supplanting the liveries of dozens of constituent companies from a still earlier period. Yet here it was now being revived as if it represented the best of bus operating tradition.

The truth was that in some ways it did. Certainly the deep red colour and cream relief conjured up a more confident age of public transport. And it was now unique, of course; there were now no other Tilling companies in similar liveries to dilute the impact.

Besides, the West Yorkshire company also had another agenda. West Yorkshire Road Car buses running in the area of the Passenger Transport Executive (itself confusingly called West Yorkshire) had been repainted into green and cream PTE livery since 1985, so in a significant part of its main operating territory the identity of the West Yorkshire company was starting to disappear. In restoring its old livery, the owners instinctively harked back to an era when the company had had a strong identity of its own; and that meant pre-NBC.

Much of the fleet was eventually painted into this new version of the Tilling scheme. It started out reasonably authentic-looking, although increasingly its gold leaf lettering was replaced by yellow. It even developed new variants to reflect the company's division into separate operations at York, Harrogate and Keighley. Its future looked fairly secure.

That prospect was ended abruptly, however, when the main company was sold to the PTE's privatised successor, Yorkshire Rider, in July 1989. Ironically, this meant that its buses now reverted to the very livery the red had been intended to fend off. Meanwhile the Keighley and Harrogate operations, although remaining independent, soon abandoned the red for new colour schemes of their own.

While these events were taking place in the north of England, a notable saga was also under way in the south. Of all the liveries in use when the corporate NBC style was imposed, the one which was probably most widely expected to be revived was that of the Southdown company. Somehow the famous apple green and cream colour scheme had never quite gone away; throughout the NBC years it seemed to make continual reappearances, either at rallies or on training buses or special vehicles of one sort or another. There was an unspoken assumption that it would be restored to general use one day.

And so it turned out to be. Although lacking the elaborate 'wild-west' fleetname of earlier years (a variety of more modern equivalents were adopted), the post-NBC version that appeared in 1985 was

nevertheless unmistakable, and restored a much-missed splash of colour to the Sussex landscape.

Moreover, in 1986 the Brighton area operations were split off into a new company, Brighton & Hove, which initially revived a version of the erstwhile Brighton Hove & District red and cream livery. However, under privatisation its new owners soon changed this for a predominantly cream colour scheme.

What brought the Southdown revival to an end was something that was to become the bane of many imaginative bus liveries: in August 1989 the company was bought by the Stagecoach group. In Southdown's case, this development was even more radical than for many of its fellow-companies. Not only did the livery disappear in favour of Stagecoach's ubiquitous white and stripe; the company name was abandoned too, as Southdown was merged with other group operations to become part of Stagecoach South.

A similar fate befell neighbouring Alder Valley (initially Alder Valley South), which was eventually broken up and shared between adjoining companies. Arguably Alder Valley's post-NBC two-tone green livery was not strictly a revival, since there had been no Alder Valley company as such before NBC — and hence no Alder Valley livery either. But there had been Aldershot & District, on whose former green livery the new one was based; it was later merged with Thames Valley (once a Tilling red company) to form Alder Valley. The new two-tone green and yellow livery, although not deeply traditional in design, had unmistakable echoes of the old Aldershot scheme. But Stagecoach took control here in 1992, and that was the end of that.

Another spurious, but arguably effective, livery 'revival' came at East Midland Motor Services, which in the immediate post-NBC era adopted a green and cream livery with clear if slightly muted echoes of the Southdown and Alder Valley schemes. The new scheme quite effectively combined a traditional image with a modern feel. However, the fate of this scheme was similar to that of the other two; it disappeared following takeover of the company by Stagecoach in 1989.

For a while it looked as though the revivalist movement was dying away. Then, as recently as 1993, Midland Red North surprised everyone by launching what was arguably the most thorough going livery revival of them all. Until then, the company's post-NBC image had been somewhat muddled, with a variety of separate identities for its various operating bases (at Telford, Cannock and so on). Arguably the identity of the core company was in danger of disappearing altogether — although latterly the company had started to unify its image by adopting a white (then yellow) and red colour scheme.

Suddenly the old Midland Red was revived as the company took on the fleetname and livery that had once belonged to the whole Midland group. The effect was strikingly convincing, and extended to gold underlined Midland fleetname and fleetnumbers. In old Midland haunts such as the area around Birmingham's New Street station it was as though 20 years had been stripped away.

In due course much of the fleet was repainted into the revived livery; but as it turned out, its life was relatively short. The company's new parent, British Bus (now Cowie) can't have failed to notice that the red was somewhat muted and unexciting. At all events, several other British Bus companies were by now introducing modern liveries with a strong yellow element, and in 1995 it was decided that something along these lines would be more in tune with the times.

It was ironical that this 'something' was more or less the same red and yellow livery that had so recently been abandoned. Arguably, though, the revival had served a purpose. The name Midland Red had been brought back into currency in a context that must have struck chords with many who remembered the original version. Midland Red North could now promote its corporate image with more assurance of credibility.

One might be forgiven for concluding from all this that anyone with the audacity to revive a long-abandoned bus livery is inevitably on a hiding to nothing. At best, the companies in question seem to change their minds fairly promptly about the revival and switch to something more modern; at worst, they get taken over and lose their identity altogether.

It is not quite true, though. One ex-NBC company which has persevered successfully with a revived livery is East Yorkshire. When the company drafted in Routemasters in 1988 to compete on city services with Hull City Transport, it also revived its pre-NBC dark blue and primrose livery. To the untutored eye the

Routemasters must have looked uncannily like the AEC Renowns and Bridgemasters that had worn the livery for real; which was precisely the effect the company wanted.

The Routemasters ran right up to 1995. They've gone now, but the old livery has been retained for the high-profile (and high-intensity) Hull services they operated. It now represents a slightly anomalous but none the less welcome local identity, and at the start of 1997 was carried by some very smartly turned-out Leyland Olympians with Northern Counties bodies. Alongside them, the main fleet now carries a maroon and cream livery, which itself has the refinement of a strongly traditional style.

As a postscript to all this, it is perhaps only fair to give some credit to the Stagecoach group. Although much criticised for the rigid imposition of its standard white livery, at least it deserves acknowledgement for the treatment it has given the buses in its East London fleet. Here it is obliged by tendering requirements to maintain a red London livery, and from the first it has done this with gusto and commitment, particularly on its Routemasters.

Not only do they seem to have more sparkle and better-maintained red paintwork than any of those in

Below:
Southdown's traditional colours were revived in the late 1980s, and very smart they were too, even with the fleetname still in NBC block lettering. Variations on the Southdown theme included the addition of the subtitle West Sussex, as on this Duple-bodied Leopard, or East & Mid Sussex.

Above left:
A Cynon Valley Bristol RE in Halifax-style colours. Halifax had in turn copied them from Glasgow.

Below left:
Dark red and an old-style fleetname on a Yorkshire Traction low-height Metrobus in Leeds in 1987

Above:
Best of the retros? An East Yorkshire Routemaster in Hull. The Routemasters have gone, but the livery lives on.

rival London fleets; they probably also have the most traditional livery. Almost as soon as it took over, Stagecoach gave them gold leaf fleetnames and fleetnumbers, and also changed the colour of the band between the decks from white to cream. No one can fault the group for conviction in what it chooses to do.

So what conclusion can we draw from the saga of the pre-NBC livery revival? Clearly, that when a corporate style is imposed from above, a strong undercurrent of support for the previous livery can survive for many years, within individual companies as well as beyond them.

Whether the former style can hold its own in a later era is less clear. Many of the revived pre-NBC liveries were cut off in their prime by further company takeovers, so the jury must be out on the question of what might have been their natural lifespan or further development. Some, however, were simply abandoned by their operators without external pressure —

suggesting perhaps that traditional liveries can sometimes simply reach the end of their useful life.

On the other hand, after the riot of diagonal stripes and generally unsympathetic livery treatments that accompanied deregulation in less fortunate fleets, you could argue that in the late 1990s bus liveries in general have become more dignified again. The yellows and reds may be brighter than in the old days, but professional designers have regained control and given them more finesse. There are still aberrations, of course — some of them quite sweeping; and wide-ranging uniformity of any kind inevitably stifles individual flair. But generally an evolutionary mood seems to have re-established itself.

Maybe to expect a straight revival of old liveries is asking too much. It seems their underlying spirit is constantly regenerating itself anyway; so perhaps we should be enjoying the substance where we find it, rather than seeking out too much detail and possibly missing the point.

Transports of Delight

Gavin Booth

Above:
The mid-engined Volvo Citybus has a higher floorline than rear-engined models. Ten delivered to Southdown in 1989 had unusually tall-looking bodies by Northern Counties. Stewart J. Brown

The big six-wheeler, scarlet-painted, London Transport, diesel-engined 97hp omnibus was, if we are being pedantic, already well past its sell-by date when Michael Flanders and Donald Swann sang about it in 'A Transport of Delight' in 1957. OK, it was maybe a touch anachronistic — the double-decker in London at the time was resolutely four-wheeled and at least 115bhp — but entertainers are permitted a bit of licence, and anyway it does suggest that there exists a great affection for double-deckers.

The trouble is, by the time the 1990s came along there were some who saw the double-decker as anachronistic. In a world now dominated by such previously unheard-of animals as minibuses and midibuses, the poor double-decker was no longer flavour of the month.

The twin '-ations' of the 1980s — deregulation and privatisation — saw to that.

Deregulation introduced a need for a quick, cheap response to competition, so hordes of the dreaded bread-vans gave operators the ideal competitive tool. The successful ones graduated to bigger minibuses, and then to midibuses. The unsuccessful ones went out of business.

Privatisation introduced a new awareness of the bottom line. Where local authorities, PTAs and benign state-owned industries tolerated a bit of waste in the interests of maintaining a dominant presence, suddenly bus companies were owned by shareholders who worried about personal profit, and cost-cutting became the order of the day.

'So what has all this to do with double-deckers?' I hear you murmur. Well, in overall cost terms the double-decker is a very efficient machine. It costs a bit more to buy — roughly 10% more than a full-size lowfloor single-decker — but is often at least as cheap to run, needing little more fuel and no more on-board staff. In maintenance terms the engine on a double-decker is often easier to get at than on a single-decker, and it takes up less space in a bus garage and indeed on congested roads.

This being so, why are operators not queuing to buy double-deckers? There are arguments about top deck security, which can cause problems in some places. There is the unassailable fact that all 70 or 80 seats are rarely occupied these days, and the slightly more contentious argument that folks are happy to get a space in a 70-*passenger* bus, even though roundly one-third of them might be required to stand.

Traffic staff in some bus companies used to love this argument. They were providing passenger *capacity* after all, and that seemed to salve their consciences. The fact that a few nights standing for 40 minutes in a crowded bus might do wonders for second-hand car sales probably never occurred to them.

All of this might be seen to suggest that Britain is devoid of double-deckers, which of course is patently untrue. But between 1985 and 1995 the double-deck population in Britain dropped by 21%, as single-deck numbers grew by 30% — the most dramatic increase being in the 17-35-seat range where the population grew by over 400%.

And there are parts of Britain where you will search long and hard to find a double-decker, or even a decent-sized single-decker, particularly in the evenings and on Sundays. The other side of the coin is that deregulation and privatisation have prolonged the life of Britain's parc of older double-deckers. Under the old rules, buses went to the great Barnsley in the sky after 12-15 years of hard service. But no more. Think about it: if you applied this rule there wouldn't be a Bristol VRT or Daimler Fleetline in service with a major operator, Atlanteans would be on their last legs, and even models that some of us regard as positively modern, like the Leyland Lion

43

and Titan, MCW Metrobus and Volvo Ailsa, should be well on the way to the dustbin of memory.

But of course that's not the case.

Stand in Birmingham's Bull Ring and among the hordes of newer single-deckers there will be lots of Metrobuses, many extensively refurbished to extend their operational lives. Stand in Edinburgh's Princes Street, and you will be surrounded by Olympians. You will believe that the double-decker has a future in

Manchester's Piccadilly, Glasgow's Argyle Street, the Headrow in Leeds — and of course London's Oxford Street. Sharing the roadway there with taxis you will see double-deckers that are considerably older: the good old Routemaster in its re-engined and refurbished form looks set to serve London into the next century — and remember that the *newest* ones date from 1968.

The shape of the 1990s double-decker was really defined way back in the 1950s when Leyland engineers designed the Atlantean, with its transverse rear engine and setback front axle. Descendants of the Atlantean (some examples of which were built as recently as 1984) and its contemporaries the Daimler Fleetline and Bristol VRT, survive, giving excellent service to this day, but these first generation rear-engined double-deckers appear ponderous and uncomfortable compared with today's equivalents with their fast-revving engines, sophisticated automatic gearboxes, and air suspension, in the same way the early rear-engined double-deckers in the 1960s seemed so modern compared with the previous generation of front-engined models.

There was a brief 'second generation' of rear-engined double-deckers, the models introduced in the 1970s to challenge Leyland's monopoly of double-deck chassis production. The apparently eccentric front-engined Ailsa seemed an unlikely contender, but went on to prove to be a hard-working and long-lived type. The Scania-MCW Metropolitan was a glimpse of the future — fast and air-suspended — but it was maybe just a bit fast for some drivers, was unpredictable on certain road surfaces, and there were corrosion problems.

The current generation was spearheaded by the Leyland Titan — air suspension, independent on the front axle, hydraulically-operated gearbox and brakes — an advanced package that was well ahead of its time and as a result frightened most buyers off. The Titan was aimed primarily at the London market, though at one time Leyland saw it as its sole double-deck model. Also aimed at London Transport, though more widely accepted, was MCW's Metrobus, an attempt to build on the limited success of the Metropolitan with a more control-

its heyday. South Yorkshire PTE kept it going during the 1980s when it adopted it as its standard model.

The seminal double-decker of the 1980s came from Leyland, and quite properly, for Leyland's Titan in 1927 and Atlantean in 1956 had redefined the double-deck concept, and the Olympian, introduced in 1980, took the Atlantean concept a significant step further. Scania also bounced into the UK double-deck market with the BR112, later the N112 and now the N113, a transverse-rear-engined underframe specially designed for the UK market.

Then Volvo adapted its successful B10M single-deck chassis to produce the Citybus, the first underfloor-engined double-decker to go into production for the UK market. Stung into action, Leyland rushed a version of a chassis built by its Danish subsidiary, DAB, into production as the Lion, and although in sales terms this was much less successful than the Citybus, it has proved to be a reliable bus. With moves towards low floors and better access, underfloor-engined double-deckers were unlikely to succeed, and both models quietly faded away after Volvo acquired Leyland.

The 1980s saw the demise of many of the familiar double-deck models — the Ailsa, Fleetline, Metropolitan, Titan and VRT — and by 1990 there were only four models available: the Citybus, Dominator, N113 and Olympian. Of these, the Olympian was clear market leader, but in a market that was severely depressed.

It was a surprise, then, when in 1991 not one but two new double-deckers arrived in this depressed market-place. Leeds-based bodybuilder Optare, which had

Above:
The Ailsa was an alternative to Leyland-built double-deckers. Eastern Scottish was one of five Scottish Bus Group subsidiaries to buy new Ailsas. All SBG Ailsas had Alexander bodies. *Stewart J. Brown*

Below:
The Leyland Olympian was the definitive 1980s double-decker and was bought by most major urban operators. Merseyside took batches with Northern Counties bodies. *Stewart J. Brown*

lable package without the need for any Swedish input.

The Dennis Dominator was a bridge between generations — a solid Fleetline replacement, initially lacking air suspension, that stayed on the model lists long after

pushed the design barriers back with its Delta model, unveiled the Spectra, based on a new DAF chassis, the rear-engined DB250, a fruit of its short-lived involvement with United Bus. The Spectra was an attractive package, and following the demise of United Bus, the DB250 has been sold with bodies by Northern Counties.

The DB250 may not have sold in earth-shattering quantities — yet — but at least it has sold, which is more than can be said for another new 1991 model, the Volvo TurboCity 100. Essentially an Italian single-deck citybus design, the one bus built, with an Alexander body, was not a happy machine and lingered on the second-hand market for some time before being bought up by Filer's of Ilfracombe.

The Olympian was Volvo-ised in 1993, and continued to outsell its rivals. Dennis quietly killed off the Dominator in favour of a new double-decker based on the Lance single-decker, the Arrow, introduced in 1995. At the same time DAF showed a lowfloor version of its DB250 chassis, relaunched in 1997 as the basis for an improved Spectra. Dennis introduced what is the first lowfloor double-decker to go into production, the three-axle Trident for export markets, and there is no doubt that this is the future for the double-decker, in the same way the single-deck market has gone uncompromisingly lowfloor. A lowfloor Volvo model for the UK was expected in 1997, and could well have been launched by the time you read this, and Dennis and Scania, both experienced in lowfloor technology, can't be far behind.

The fact that manufacturers are so keen to invest in new double-deck models indicates that they see a future for the breed. Export considerations play a significant part in all this, of course, but reports of the death of the UK double-deck market will surely prove to be an exaggeration, to paraphrase the words of Mark Twain.

The engines fitted to double-deckers have tended to be big, both in physical size and output. The Gardner 6LX family, beloved of engineers and accountants, was one of the strong selling-points for the Daimler Fleetline, and when the Fleetline seemed to be on the way out, Dennis offered the Dominator as a Gardner-engined replacement — though interestingly the biggest Dominator customer, the South Yorkshire PTE, opted for Rolls-Royce engines. The Foden double-decker of the same period was Gardner-powered, though it never got beyond the prototype stage.

The amalgamation of so many companies under the British Leyland banner led to what had previously seemed unthinkable — Leyland engines in Daimler Fleetlines and Bristol VRTs, and Gardner engines in Leyland Titans. Although Daimler had offered other engine types in its model range, Leyland had previously never sold its engines for fitting in rival models — and with its own comprehensive engine range, Leyland would never have dreamed of fitting anything else.

When the Olympian came along, Leyland offered its own TL11 engine for Leyland customers, and the Gardner 6LXB for traditional Gardner fans. Later, when the TL11 had been stretched as far as it could go, and Leyland engine-building closed down, the Cummins L10 was offered in the Olympian, and the L10 with the ZF automatic gearbox became a popular combination. Following the introduction of the Volvo Olympian, the L10 was phased out in favour of Volvo's own D10A unit.

The reorganisation of the British bus industry following privatisation has concentrated buying power in a small number of hands, and manufacturers rely on the volume business from the supergroups to shore up the smaller orders from everybody else.

In the darkest days of the late 1980s Stagecoach beamed a shaft of light by ordering new buses, including double-deckers, and it has gone on with regular, growing, orders where double-deckers have always had their place. The Stagecoach choice is the Olympian, with bodywork by Alexander and Northern Counties.

FirstBus was more of a problem. Its two constituents, Badgerline and GRT, had no great track record with double-deckers, and for a time it looked as if FirstBus would pursue an all-single-deck line. But its 1996-announced orders included double-deckers — Alexander-bodied Olympians — and it looks as if it recognises that there is still a role for double-deckers.

British Bus had no clear buying policy, and as this is written it is not clear what position Cowie will adopt. Certainly Cowie has a fast-track to DAF models through its Hughes-DAF subsidiary, and it will be interesting to see if the DB250 becomes the group's standard model.

Some former double-deck strongholds are showing few signs of ordering more. As PTEs, Merseyside, South Yorkshire and West Midlands were major double-deck customers, but their privatised successors appear to be moving heavily towards single-deckers. It is left to some of the few remaining publicly-owned fleets, most notably Lothian, to keep the double-deck flag flying; Lothian has faithfully bought 30-plus long-wheelbase Olympians most years since the late 1980s.

The sad fact, for those of us who admire the double-decker, is that the population is dropping. Taking figures from the 1990 and 1996 editions of *The Little Red Book*, we find that the emphasis is shifting firmly in favour of single-deckers of all sizes.

Looking at 10 once-major double-deck fleets we find that there are 21% fewer double-deckers over the six years and 57% more single-deckers. The biggest double-

Top left:
The last decade has seen a steady increase in the number of single-deck buses on Britain's roads. The Volvo B10B has been a popular choice in a number of fleets. Wright bodywork is fitted to this West Riding bus, photographed at Meadowhall bus station. Stewart J. Brown

Centre left:
Double-deckers in the 1990s have evolved with new style. The Optare Spectra, based on the DAF DB250, was a trend-setter. Wilts & Dorset is the biggest user of Spectras. Stewart J. Brown

Bottom left:
East Lancs teamed up with Scania to introduce the Cityzen in 1995. Buyers have included Mayne of Manchester, Brighton & Hove and, as seen in Newcastle, Northumbria. Stewart J. Brown

Right:
A new double-deck chassis from Dennis, the Arrow, first entered service in 1996. Capital Citybus is the biggest Arrow user. Northern Counties Palatine II bodywork is fitted to this bus, liveried for an Underground replacement service. Stewart J. Brown

deck drops are at Merseyside (down 37%), Mainline and Nottingham (down 34% each) and Busways (down 29%), while even at Lothian the number has dropped by 8% and only Strathclyde has stayed constant. The biggest jumps in the single-deck population have been at West Midlands (an amazing 268%) and Mainline (up 59%). Overall, the ratio of double-deck to single-deck buses in these fleets, has changed dramatically. In 1990 it was 81:19, but by 1996 it was 68:32.

These are the main fleets outside London that tended to favour double-deckers in the past. In London, the double-deck parc has dropped by 25%, the single-deck numbers have literally doubled, and the dd:sd ratio changed from 86:14 in 1990 to 70:30 six years later.

On the other hand, the company fleets, formerly part of NBC or SBG, tended to have fewer double-deck buses anyway. In 1990 the dd:sd ratio was roundly

40:60, and in 1996 it was 34:66. Some fleets have bought few, if any, double-deckers in that time: the double-deck populations at City of Oxford, Eastern National, South Wales, Trent, West Riding and Yorkshire Traction have dropped significantly. Most other fleets have fewer double-deckers now, but a handful — Cambus, East Yorkshire, Midland Fox, United Counties — now have more double-deckers than in 1990.

Although the double-decker is not a uniquely British animal — it still thrives in Berlin, Hong Kong and Singapore — Britain still has by far the biggest double-deck population in the world. Fears that the very existence of the double-decker could be threatened by European legislation appear to be unfounded, though the various Euro regulations on emissions have resulted in greener and more environmentally-friendly models.

The articulated bus has often been put forward as an alternative to the double-decker, and its proponents often cite the crowd-moving properties of artics in European cities — usually in buses where the standing capacity greatly outnumbers the seating capacity, it must be said. The counter-argument is that the double-decker is economical on urban road-space, offers a high proportion of seating space, and that Britain is largely designed to present few overhead obstructions to a 4.5m high bus.

So the double-decker has a future, even in a more restricted role than before. The Dennis Arrow with its in-line Cummins C-series engine has challenged the transverse-engine concept, and it may be that we shall see more compact, but still gutsy, engines in future

Above:
Lothian has standardised on the long-wheelbase Olympian. Initially built by Leyland, more recent deliveries have been produced at Volvo's Scottish plant in Irvine. This is a Leyland Olympian which, like most Lothian buses, has Alexander bodywork. Stewart J. Brown

Below:
An artist's impression of Alexander's new double-deck body, the ALX400. The first production examples are due in service in 1998. Alexander

models, and we shall certainly see a move to the lowfloor layout. After all, double-deckers pioneered the concept. What was the Bristol Lodekka if not a lowfloor double-decker nearly half-a-century ahead of its time?

ALX400
low entry UK decker

Lost Soulmates

For small operators local bus deregulation opened up new opportunities —
or threatened their very existence. **Alan Millar** looks at old-established
companies which have vanished or sold out since 1986.

Scratch the soul of a *Buses Yearbook* reader and there's a strong chance of uncovering a deep affection for independent operators. Especially the ones running what used to be called stage carriage services in urban areas with double-deckers, distinctive liveries and tickets with the company's name printed on them.

If you're over a certain age, your affection will be stronger if the double-deckers once had front engines, half cabs and exposed radiators and were bought new and second-hand from a variety of sources, but it won't be wiped out by more modern buses with rear engines or even without top decks. Nor by the occasionally ropey

state of some of the vehicles. For it's the independence that matters most, that makes these smaller fleets stand out from the private sector giants of today or the state-owned groups of the past. Our love of the underdog pitches independents into a special place in our hearts as plucky battlers against potentially boring operators of masses of identically painted identical vehicles.

So, even if we entertained misgivings when Nicholas Ridley was preparing to deregulate the bus industry in 1985, I guess many of us hoped independents might blossom in the new regime. After half a century of being constrained by road service licensing, perhaps they would start the extra routes that the big boys had always stopped them from running before. That was the romantic view. In reality, regulation protected most independent stage carriage operators more than it restricted them and many were genuinely worried by the Ridley revolution. On one hand, they could be preyed upon by big operators and, on the other, they became vulnerable to attack by lower cost, smaller, newer and, in

Below:
Small bus operators have been prey for bigger businesses since bus operation began. In the 1960s the Scottish Bus Group took over a number of small fleets including Burnett of Mintlaw. A Harrington-bodied AEC Reliance in Burnett livery carries an Alexander (Northern) fleetnumber soon after Northern bought the Burnett company. Stewart J. Brown

some cases, more commercially astute companies. Other predators were under-resourced, poor quality enterprises operating on the edges of legality.

All of which has been enough to persuade many traditional, pre-deregulation stage carriage independents to throw in the towel and, since 1986, many of the best-loved examples of the breed have either vanished altogether or survive in name only as trading wings of larger businesses.

Not, of course, that they weren't endangered before. Family firms depend on younger generations being prepared — and able — to continue their parents' and grandparents' businesses. There are inheritance tax bills to pay when founders die and problems also arise if the older generations have not made adequate provision for retirement pensions and continue to draw income from profits which must also provide a living for the younger directors and, hopefully, fund the renewal of assets. Occasions also arise when a business or the property it occupies is more valuable to a potential buyer than it is to the owners. All these factors, and a combination of bus industry restructures and gradually declining passenger numbers, have contributed to a steady attrition among the ranks of independents over the decades. As far back as 1933/34, London Transport was compulsorily acquiring local bus operators. In the 1960s, the Scottish Bus Group wiped out whole swathes of independent activity, notably in Lanarkshire and Aberdeenshire. And in the 1970s, Midland Red bought Harper of Heath Hayes, Green Bus of Rugeley and a clutch of Telford operators while the South Yorkshire PTE waved such tempting cheques before the Doncaster independents that most sold their buses.

Indeed, there were substantial parts of the country which had long since lost their independent services in 1986. That helps explain why the possibilities of tendered and commercial bus operation held out limited appeal to the survivors of businesses dating back to the 1920s and 1930s and why many were prepared to accept takeover terms offered by newly privatised National Bus Company subsidiaries and surviving municipals. In southeast England, the already thin independent ranks were pruned substantially when Red Rover of Aylesbury and Premier Travel of Cambridge sold out early in 1988. Red Rover, in Aylesbury since 1928 and latterly running 22 vehicles on commercial and recently-won tendered routes, was bought by employee-owned Luton & District in January 1988. The Red Rover name was retained for a short time, but the separate livery and acquired vehicles didn't last long. It had been a keen buyer of London Transport RT, RTL and RTW double-deckers, graduating on to new AEC Bridgemasters and a Renown in the 1960s and bought four Optare CityPacer minibuses in 1986/87, but much of its big bus fleet was second-hand at the end — a mix mostly of Leyland Nationals, ex-LT DMS-class Fleetlines and some uncannily similar South Yorkshire machines.

Premier's fate was more complex. Formed in 1936, it

Top:
The silver and blue livery used by Cambridge Coach Services is substantially unaltered from that used by Premier in its final independent days. Park of Hamilton was the first owner of this Volvo B10M with Plaxton Paramount 3500 body. *Alan Millar*

Above:
South Notts bought new double-deckers, standardising on Fleetlines with Northern Counties bodies. This is a 1991 view, after ownership of the company had passed to Nottingham City Transport. It carries NCT legal lettering and an NCT fleetnumber — 195 — above the door which conflicts with its original number, 115, still displayed on the front. *Alan Millar*

grew to run around 90 vehicles on a mix of local bus routes, express services (some latterly on behalf of National Express) and more general coach work. It also had a thriving travel agency chain which accounted for nearly 90% of the total business and, when three directors sold their shareholdings in 1987, the remaining board members opted to sell the buses and coaches and concentrate on selling holidays.

It looked like newly privatised Cambus would get the buses and coaches, but an 11th hour revolt in the ranks led managers to team up with another ex-NBC management team, the AJS Group, which had acquired West Yorkshire Road Car and was in the process of buying London Country (North East). The new owners started refocusing the business, pulling out of underperforming general coaching and school contracts

and starting to compete against Cambus with new bus routes.

The head-to-head competition diminished quickly and AJS began reviewing its own future after missing out on the chances of buying Southdown and Eastern National in 1989/90. It was soon selling off its businesses and Cambus finally got 63 of Premier's vehicles in May 1990 along with all the local bus services, the National Express contracts and some general coaching work. The Premier name was retained for all of Cambus Holdings' coach work, but in a new livery style, and even that fleet was halved to around 30 coaches after Stagecoach took over these businesses at the end of 1995.

AJS retained the old Premier livery style on 16 coaches run primarily on express services from Cambridge to the London airports, renaming that operation as Cambridge Coach Services and finally selling it to Blazefield Holdings, a management buy-out from part of AJS, in November 1991. Subsequently expanded, this is probably the most recognisable remnant of the old Premier company, even if it doesn't bear its name.

At least these businesses were taken over. After 70 years on the streets of Windsor, A. Moore & Sons' Imperial Bus Services closed down in January 1987 and its brown and cream fleet of 13 Fords and Bedfords passed into history. In deregulated Britain, it was no longer necessary to buy a company if you wanted to run its routes.

One of the largest independents in southwest England, Bere Regis Coaches, survived until 1995. It sold 28 coaches and minibuses — about three-quarters of the total business — to Cawlett Holdings (management-owned Southern National/North Devon) in March 1994 along with its Dorchester depot. The rest of the company closed down quietly 18 months later. Cawlett changed the company name to West Dorset Coaches, but adopted Dorchester Coachways as its fleetname and gave the acquired vehicles a modern, orange-based livery.

Some of the biggest takeovers have been in the Midlands. Indeed, the biggest surviving pre-deregulation independent, loss-making Barton, was acquired in July 1989 by Wellglade, the management team which bought Trent at the end of 1986. In NBC days, Trent had held a small shareholding in Barton which ran 211 bus grant coaches across large parts of Nottinghamshire, Derbyshire and Leicestershire, largely overlapping Trent's territory. Under the deal, Wellglade got the vehicles, services and Barton Buses name, not the stock market-listed company itself which had once been

involved in haulage and retained the property. The fleet was almost immediately trimmed back to 180 vehicles and most of it was moved into Trent's depots, but the Barton brand was retained and, for a time, smoking was permitted on Barton buses while it was banned on Trent's. Today, Wellglade uses Barton red and cream as its fleet colours, and continues to distinguish between Trent and Barton fleetnames.

Despite the clear strengths of the 81-year-old Barton name, Trent's directors realised that they had inherited a business with many weaknesses common to independent, family-owned companies. It had few managers and even fewer with much experience beyond Barton; and labour relations were largely unstructured, with employees bypassing their immediate superiors and solving grievances with family members.

Its fleet was disproportionately old. Cleverly, Barton had taken advantage of the bus grant scheme and replaced its extraordinarily assorted fleet of single-deckers and lowbridge Leyland and AEC double-deckers with dual-purpose coaches in the early 1970s. Unfortunately, it hadn't maintained the pace of renewal

and over a third of the 1989 fleet comprised 15- and 16-year-old Leyland Leopards; there also were newer but troublesome Tigers which Wellglade disposed of with great alacrity.

An even worse situation presented itself in east Nottinghamshire after Yorkshire Traction, which had just bought Lincolnshire Road Car from NBC, bought Gash of Newark in March 1988. Gash — a typical business from the years immediately after World War 1 — was the stuff of enthusiasts' fantasies, running an immaculate fleet of exposed radiator Daimlers long after most other operators had dispatched theirs for scrap and it applied the same smart two-tone green livery to newer single-deckers like Leopards and rare Marshall-bodied Bristol LHSs.

But it greatly overstretched itself after deregulation, bidding successfully for more tendered services than it could handle and virtually doubling the fleet with a mix of second-hand vehicles (including Leyland Atlanteans, Bristol REs and AEC Routemasters). Its first rear-engined buses included some rough specimens that would have tried a more experienced operator's patience, never mind one with little idea of what to expect. The maintenance problems persisted and, to Yorkshire Traction's embarrassment, the Traffic Commissioner revoked Gash's operator's licence a year after the takeover, but increased Road Car's vehicle allowance by an equivalent figure. Road Car let the Gash name die, but turned the old company into its in-house advertising business.

Below:
South Yorkshire's unusual livery on a Northern Counties-bodied Fleetline in Leeds in 1980, when independents were largely protected by the road service licensing system. South Yorkshire is now part of the Cowie Group. Stewart J. Brown

Above:
Trimdon Motor Services used the Bristol LH to launch new companies and services in the northeast of England. When this photograph was taken in 1991, TMS, Trimdon's Teesside offshoot, had been sold to Caldaire. *Alan Millar*

Another inheritance of older buses came a big operator's way in March 1991 when council-owned Nottingham City Transport took over the 29-vehicle South Notts Bus Company, based at Gotham and running between Loughborough and Nottingham. Formed in 1926 and 50% owned by Barton from 1929, South Notts needed lowheight double-deckers to pass under a subsequently demolished bridge in Wilford Lane and to fit into its unmodified garage. In latter years, it bought Northern Counties and ECW-bodied Fleetlines and took delivery of two Northern Counties Olympians in 1989, but had also begun buying second-hand.

It had run routes jointly with Nottingham and, when it existed, West Bridgford UDC from 1952, sharing in the huge market for travel to and from the city's Clifton housing estate which, reputedly, was Europe's largest. New competition had come on the scene in 1990 in the shape of Kinch's of Loughborough and it appears that Nottingham snapped up South Notts — which started losing money — to stop it being bought by Kinch.

Nottingham kept the traditional blue and cream livery (minus the maroon it also used to wear), but started cascading mid-life buses from the main city fleet and later bought some highly unusual long-wheelbase East Lancs-bodied Olympians

In Staffordshire, PMT — as privatised Potteries Motor Traction somewhat insensitively renamed itself in an age when the initials are better understood as an uncomfortable female complaint — bought up the remnants of Berresford of Cheddleton and its Stonier's subsidiary in June 1987 following the proprietor's death and went on to buy long-established Turner of Brown

Edge the following November when its proprietors retired. The Turner identity was retained. In September 1989, it took over the similarly long-lived bus services of Poole's of Alsager Bank which had come within a whisker of being bought by Berresford's.

A little farther south, Stevenson's of Uttoxeter seemed to defy gravity. Pursuing the belief that businesses either expand or die, it had taken over the East Staffordshire municipal fleet in Burton upon Trent in 1985, bought into Midland Fox (and took over its Swadlincote depot), acquired some smaller neighbours and established itself as a potent competitor in the West Midlands conurbation. Along the way, it had also been in and out of Greater Manchester and had expanded from a respectable fleet strength of 50 in 1984 to the dizzy heights of 270 extraordinarily assorted new and often low-mileage second-hand vehicles.

Then West Midlands Travel launched itself into Burton. Too much for a possibly overstretched business, Stevenson's sold out to British Bus in June 1994 and soon pulled out of most of the West Midlands while WMT withdrew again from Burton. Under new ownership, Stevenson's survives, but in place of their separate red and yellow liveries, it shares a common yellow and red scheme with Midland Red North with only a fleetname to tell them apart. Perhaps in compensation, it was given responsibility for Midland Red's Cheshire services which were hardly in the Midlands.

Longer-established independents have fared little better across northern England. In June 1988, South Yorkshire Transport, as today's Mainline then styled itself, acquired the 13 vehicles of one of the few surviving Doncaster independents — Premier of Stainforth. Premier had been the trading name of Harold Wilson Ltd for decades before a more famous Harold Wilson became Britain's prime minister in 1964. It ran from Doncaster to Goole and Moorend, latterly with vehicles that included an early Alexander-bodied Ailsa, three Atlanteans and a pair of ex-Tayside Bristol VRTs.

Six years later, in July 1994, a much smaller South Yorkshire was taken over. Caldaire Holdings (owner of ex-NBC West Riding and Yorkshire Woollen) snapped up the 18-vehicle, Pontefract-based South Yorkshire Road Transport whose blue and white buses served the once thriving mining communities on routes stretching as far as Doncaster and Leeds. The company's titles (it had previously been South Yorkshire Motors) always made it sound as though it was a much bigger business and, almost to the end of its independence, it continued buying new lowheight double-deckers, latterly Northern Counties-bodied Olympians.

At some point in the early 1970s, someone persuaded the company that it would be a great idea to paint the fleet in blocks of blues and white instead of the traditional bands of blues and cream found on earlier generations of lowbridge Leylands and Albions. It's a dangerous practice to pass judgement on something so subjective as a livery, but one can see why local writers Michael Fowler and Tony Peart were moved a few years ago to comment that 'a present-day South Yorkshire Olympian still looks like a huge carton of washing powder on wheels'.

Caldaire kept South Yorkshire as a separate entity, but changed the livery layout to its more bus-like corporate style. This was further simplified after British Bus took over in 1995. The fleet has been replaced with new and cascaded vehicles, but at least the company survives as an identifiable, if diluted, reminder of its independent past.

Which is more than can be said of Connor & Graham of Easington, whose long-established bus services (started in 1926) from Easington and Withernsea into Hull were taken over by East Yorkshire Motor Services in February 1993 at a time when EYMS was buying up post-deregulation independents and throwing its weight

into a competitive battle with Kingston upon Hull City Transport. Two Atlanteans and a Fleetline went in that deal and in May 1994 the company's 14 remaining private hire and contract vehicles were also taken over.

On the west side of the Pennines, EYMS bought 41-vehicle Finglands of Manchester in May 1991 and proceeded to build it up from being a coach operator that had begun running buses for Manchester's huge student population in the last few years before deregulation to a more substantial operator with increasing numbers of new buses. It owed part of its growth to EYMS's ability to do business with Stagecoach and take over bits of businesses that no longer fitted into that group's grand plans.

These takeovers were but chicken-feed compared with the changes further northeast where the emerging giants of the new age industry bought up some of the best known and respected names on the sides of the buses of County Durham, Northumberland and Tyne & Wear. Few single events have emphasised the pace of change as much as the Go-Ahead Group's purchase of OK Motor Services in March 1995. Founded in 1912, a year before Go-Ahead's own Northern General, Bishop Auckland-based OK had once been a co-operative of smaller operators and pandered to enthusiasts' fancies with a fine mix of single- and double-deckers bought new and, astutely, second-hand — all of them painted in a distinctive two-tone red and cream livery.

By 1986, the fleet had grown modestly to about 70 buses and coaches, some of them on regular journeys into central Newcastle. It exploited the commercial and tendered service opportunities presented by deregulation, built a depot in Peterlee new town in 1989 and had

Above
OK was another old-established company to expand rapidly after deregulation, latterly by purchasing new Volvos and Mercedes. The Volvos included B10Bs with Alexander Strider bodies. Stewart J. Brown

Below:
In 1990 Graham's Bus Service of Paisley simply vanished. The company had once had a strong presence in the Paisley area, and had been a regular buyer of new double-deckers — mainly Guy Arabs, Daimler Fleetlines and, as seen here at Linwood, Leyland Atlanteans. Roe built the body. Stewart J. Brown

almost tripled its fleet by the time Go-Ahead took over. Much of that growth had been achieved with second-hand purchases (mainly Leyland Leopards and Atlanteans, but also a unique rear-engined Tiger export development bus with an ECW body), although OK's last year and a half of independence had seen it buy nearly 50 new Mercedes and Volvo single-deckers.

New vehicles don't always appear to be the most reliable indication of the health of a bus operator and when the Monopolies and Mergers Commission cleared

the OK takeover, it commented that the company was financially weak and unlikely to be able to survive as an independent business. Under Go-Ahead ownership, OK retained its identity and was given responsibility for the 17-strong cross-Tyne Low Fell business taken over in June 1991 as well as Go-Ahead's Voyager coach unit.

This fitted in with Go-Ahead's policy of retaining the identities of other County Durham companies it acquired. None was as old or large as OK, but several had been around since the mid-1920s. Following the owner's retirement, it bought six-vehicle Gypsy Queen, otherwise known as the Langley Park Motor Company, in May 1989; J. H. Hammell's six-vehicle Diamond Service of Stanley, once a co-operative association of nine operators, followed in January 1995; and, five months later, Armstrong's of Ebchester was taken over along with 14 vehicles.

In December 1989, management-owned Northumbria bought the 50-vehicle operations of Moor-Dale of Newcastle and its R&M (formerly Rochester & Marshall) subsidiary which had been owned since 1975. Moor-Dale had expanded its bus operations after deregulation and had been owned by one Eddie Dunn, nephew of the Armstrongs who owned Armstrong Galley until 1973. R&M lost its identity soon after British Bus bought Northumbria in July 1994, but two former Northumbria directors bought the Moor-Dale coach business and made it independent again, proving that there can sometimes be life after a takeover. Around this time, Northumbria bought Hunter's of Seaton Delaval, long associated with the North Shields-Whitley Bay route. Hunter's name and its brown and cream livery were kept for 19 vehicles, but the fleet was updated with transferred stock that included Leyland Lynxes new to Moor-Dale. And in April 1996, when its 83-year-old owner retired, Raisbeck of Bedlington sold out its town service to Northumbria, but none of its three vehicles (unchanged for 11 years and including the only British example of Volvo's lightweight mid-engined B7M) were kept.

Faced with the might of Stagecoach-owned Busways on its 73-year-old route into Sunderland, W. H. Jolly of South Hylton pulled its eight Bedfords off the road in June 1995 and, four months later, United Auto (then owned by West Midlands Travel) bought the 17-vehicle business of The Eden of West Auckland, another County Durham company dating back to the 1920s.

Under Caldaire ownership, United had already absorbed a rather larger independent founded in the mid-1920s. This was Trimdon Motor Services which began a 30-year run of sometimes spectacular growth when entrepreneur Robert Lewis bought the company in 1959. He turned from second-hand buses to new Fords and, later, Leyland Leopards and Tigers, and expanded within the constraints of the licensing system, adding some new routes, but also acquiring Jersey Motor Transport, Norfolk Motor Services, Heaps Tours of Leeds and Blue Line's Newcastle-London services, before scaling down or selling many of these peripheral interests to take

advantage of deregulation opportunities on his doorstep. He prepared by buying large numbers of ex-NBC Bristol LHs during 1985 and launched his first assault, against Cleveland Transit in Stockton, in October 1986. Second-hand Leopards and Nationals followed and over 50 TMS (for Teesside Motor Services) buses were running in the area by the following year. The battles opened on to a second front in August 1987 with the 40-vehicle launch of the Tyne & Wear Omnibus Company (TWOC) subsidiary, based in Gateshead and running against Busways in Newcastle. This subsequently more than doubled in size and Busways' fight back included a couple of routes in the heart of Trimdon's traditional County Durham territory.

Trimdon's initial strength also became one of its bigger weaknesses. The LH. Its designers had never envisaged this rural bus being run on intensive urban routes and the TWOC fleet in particular was straining close to, if not beyond, its limits. The cost of buying decent replacements, combined with the low profit margins earned against surprisingly strong competition, prompted Robert Lewis to sell out before his profits turned bad. TWOC went to Go-Ahead in November 1989, but it was sold on within minutes to Busways and virtually closed down.

Caldaire bought the remaining 120 buses in March 1990, keeping the Teesside fleet and a version of its blue and white livery as a separate entity, but absorbing the original Trimdon operation into United. In one of the many bizarre twists of fate dealt by the competition authorities, the Monopolies and Mergers Commission wanted United to sell off the County Durham business again but, after lengthy lobbying, the Government eventually backed off.

With relatively few pre-deregulation independents left in business by 1986, Scotland has lost fewer old names. On Tayside, Stagecoach (itself a pre-deregulation independent rapidly shedding the chrysalis of small-time operation as it prepared to fly into an almost unimaginable world of global big-time buses) had bought McLennan's of Spittalfield in 1985. It was also believed to have considered buying Greyhound of Arbroath, which had grown up in the early 1960s by a series of acquisitions, operated various routes in Dundee and Angus with a mainly second-hand fleet of red and cream buses well past their first flush of youth and was owned by a member of the Alexander family of coachbuilding and Scottish Bus Group fame.

Instead, Greyhound gave up running bus routes when SBG's Strathtay company registered the same services in 1986 and it sold the 14 remaining coaches to Tayside Buses — then still in council ownership — in August 1990. Tayside kept the Greyhound name for its coach fleet and later adopted the racing dog logo for its buses. In the same general area, 16-vehicle Meffan of Kirriemuir was bought by Yorkshire Traction (by then the owner of Strathtay) in October 1993 while, farther south, the eight-vehicle East Lothian operator, Wiles of Port Seton, closed down at the end of 1989 after 65 years, a victim of deregulated competition and closure of local mines.

The biggest casualties have been in the West of Scotland independent heartlands of Paisley and Ayrshire. Graham's of Paisley, the larger of the two survivors of a once kaleidoscopic variety of colourful independents serving the area directly southwest of Glasgow, vanished at the end of April 1990 in particularly distressing circumstances.

The company had been around since 1929, adopted a distinctive and well-presented orange and ivory livery in the early 1950s and graduated from new and second-hand Guy Arabs to Fleetlines and Atlanteans, later a mix of mainly Leyland and Volvo single-deckers. It was still expanding in the early 1980s, establishing new routes and working hard at keeping its old ones and was running over 30 vehicles in its latter years.

But its family directors lost heart with deregulation and, seeing new and established operators registering additional routes, put the business up for sale. There were no takers. Strathclyde Buses and (briefly) Western Scottish both registered over its routes, Strathclyde took on most of the drivers and, on payment of redundancy cheques two-and-a-half days before the scheduled end of services, the drivers walked off without warning and Graham's evaporated into history. Strathclyde bought four of its Volvo B10M buses (three of them rare Caetano Stagecoaches), but gave up some of the old Graham routes in November 1993 when it exchanged routes with Clydeside 2000.

In Ayrshire, the new order has ended independent local bus operation by the three co-operatives that dominated services through the west of the county from the late 1920s. In January 1995, Stagecoach — which had bought Western Scottish and the independent Arran Coaches a few months earlier — paid over £4 million for A1 Service, the 100-vehicle operator of a network of services, most of them along the urban corridor between Kilmarnock, Irvine and Ardrossan.

A1 had been the original co-operative of small Ayrshire operators and was the only survivor in joint ownership, although the number of shareholders had fallen from 21 to nine in 60 years. That mix of ownership meant that, although the company could and did buy new and used buses in bulk, individual preferences were also met by one-off purchases and there was some considerable latitude allowed in the application of the corporate colours of blue, white and maroon. Even more than OK, A1's policies pandered to enthusiasts' fondness for variety, with amazing selections of Leyland, AEC, Daimler and other double-deckers presenting themselves on its high frequency routes.

Its big purchases of ex-London RTs and RTLs were followed by new half-cabs with relatively common (eg Northern Counties and Massey) and less common (eg Strachans) bodywork, later by Atlanteans, Fleetlines, Ailsas and other exotica part funded by new bus grants. Latterly, its fleet became old, standards slipped and a stiff public warning from the Traffic Commissioner about vehicle maintenance ought to have been a sign that things were not as watertight as they had once been. Stagecoach's offer came as some members were considering selling up and it bettered anything that their fellow directors could afford.

Below:
A1 of Ardrossan was bought by Stagecoach at the start of 1995, and most of its existing fleet was quickly replaced by Volvo Olympians and ex-London Titans. These ousted such typical A1 buses as Alexander-bodied Ailsas. A1's blue and cream livery was revived at the end of 1996 for the company's trunk Kilmarnock to Irvine service. Stewart J. Brown

This time, the company survived but its identity was initially swept aside to make way for Stagecoach's corporate stripes. The process was accelerated by two circumstances of the sale. One was that some members hung on to some of their vehicles, leaving Stagecoach at least 15 vehicles short of requirements; the other was that the aged fleet was in such poor condition that many vehicles were rapidly taken out of service and a mix of new and mid-life buses was drafted in to replace them.

About six months after the takeover, A1 took over the bus routes of Clyde Coast, a former co-operative formed in 1928 by a breakaway from A1 and latterly running minibuses, while some of A1's contract double-deckers went to Clyde Coast. AA, the third of the former co-operatives (now owned exclusively by Dodds of Troon) initially escaped takeover and found a way of working alongside Stagecoach. It eventually sold out in the spring of 1997.

But A1's spirit hasn't been broken. Quite quickly, Stagecoach replaced corporate style fleetnames with more prominent A1 Service names in block letters. Then, towards the end of 1996, as MMC diktat compelled it to release former owners from covenants preventing them from competing against their old company, Stagecoach reinstated the old blue livery as a form of route branding for double-deckers on the main service.

It was almost as if nothing had changed — except that the buses were substantially newer than at any time in the company's history. They were also less varied, but that's what you get as part of an efficient modern business.

Other older established Scottish independents which have given up the battle have included two distantly related Irvine's businesses in Lanarkshire. Irvine's Golden Eagle of Salsburgh sold its bus routes and four vehicles to ex-SBG Kelvin Central in October 1994, and Irvine's of Law sold its route and two vehicles around a year later. In Argyllshire, West Coast of Campbeltown still looked independent to the outside world but, from late 1995, it was 25% owned by National Express.

In Wales, several post-deregulation takeovers have been effected by a pre-deregulation independent that lost its independence. The Brewer family of Caerau sold its 34-vehicle fleet to the management owners of ex-NBC South Wales Transport in January 1988. The name was kept, but the livery was changed from turquoise, dark blue and cream to red, white and yellow and the new owners started building Brewers up into something much bigger. By the end of 1988, it had taken over Llynfi Motors of Maesteg and Morris Bros of Swansea and went on to take over parts of SWT itself, the collapsed ex-NBC National Welsh and an offshoot of Cardiff Bus. Now part of FirstBus, its fleet numbers over 150.

Around Cardiff, Thomas Motor Services of Barry sold out to Shamrock Travel of Pontypridd, one of the most rapidly expanded post-deregulation independents.

Against all this retrenchment by the old guard, it's only fair to say that many newcomers have come on the scene and have survived, although its equally fair to point out that many newcomers have also disappeared or sold out. And some old-established businesses were still trading at the time of writing (January 1997) — Felix of Stanley in Derbyshire, Bond Bros of Willington and Weardale of Stanhope in County Durham, McGill's of Barrhead in Renfrewshire (the last old generation Paisley independent), Stokes of Carstairs and Hutchison of Overtown in Lanarkshire, Leon of Finningley (the last of the old Doncaster operators), Fishwick of Leyland in Lancashire, Cottrell's of Mitcheldean in Gloucestershire and Tillingbourne in Surrey to name but a few.

More remarkable have been the exceptional examples of pre-deregulation independents which have grown over the past 12 years, like Mayne's of Manchester and Hedingham Omnibuses in Essex. No one can forecast what the future will hold, but I'll wager that the souls of tomorrow's *Yearbook* readers will be etched with images of today's surviving independents — regardless of what types of vehicles they operate.

Above:
Ex-London buses had long been a feature of A1's operations. Nobody would have predicted that they would reappear when the company lost its independence. Titans transferred from Stagecoach's London businesses helped modernise the A1 fleet in 1995. One loads at Irvine Cross. Stewart J. Brown

Left:
The Atlantean was the standard choice for many local authority fleets, including Grampian Regional Transport, which took AN68s with Alexander bodies until 1983. This 1977 bus is seen in Aberdeen's Union Street in 1991.
ALL PHOTOGRAPHS BY THE AUTHOR

Going, Going,

Almost Gone...

Old buses, like old soldiers, fade away. **Stewart J. Brown** looks at some types which are fast disappearing.

Much that changes does so imperceptibly, and that's as true of bus fleets — generally — as of anything else. New buses come; old buses go. And the last few years have seen an increase in the rate of new bus deliveries, which in turn means the more rapid withdrawal of older types. Not before time, some would say, casting a jaundiced eye over smoking Leyland Nationals.

Heavy-duty buses typically have a design life of around 15 years. That has long been something of an industry norm, although with many exceptions. Apply the 15-year rule to London's Routemasters and the last would have been withdrawn in 1983...

The Routemasters may be soldiering on, but the late 1990s are going to see the disappearance from major fleets of a number of types which have been around for a very long time. The most obvious candidates for early release from front-line service with major operators are the rear-engined double-deck models which were the mainstay of most British fleets in the 1970s — the Bristol VRT, Daimler (or Leyland) Fleetline and Leyland Atlantean.

The last VRTs to enter service were X-registered buses for Northampton Transport at the start of 1982. The last Fleetlines, for Cleveland Transit, were Y-registered buses in 1983. The last Atlanteans entered service in 1984, and included a few with B-prefix registrations. All of these models are living on borrowed time. The same applies to Leyland's Leopard.

It was gradually replaced by the Tiger from 1981 — so gradually that the very last Leopards didn't actually enter service until 1984. And while Leopards in some fleets may seem to have found the bus equivalent of immortality, don't be fooled — they too are on the way out, heading slowly to that great bus garage in the sky whence they never return.

The thing about those models which were once commonplace is that they quietly fade away, often unnoticed and usually with no razzmatazz. One day the streets of Glasgow will seem to be packed with Atlanteans. Next day they'll be gone. Mark my words. And it's not just Glasgow. The same applies in every other town or city which was characterised by a particular type, whether it be Fleetlines in Derby, Atlanteans in Manchester or VRTs in Norwich. They are slowly but surely vanishing, being replaced by models which were unthought of when they entered service fresh from the factory 15 years ago — Volvo Olympians, Dennis Darts, Scania L113s, Optare Excels.

The Fleetline enjoyed high sales until 1978, boosted of course by London Transport's orders. In the mid-1970s around 650 new Fleetlines were entering service with British operators each year. London was the biggest

Above:
A number of municipal fleets bought VRTs, including Great Yarmouth, which specified lowheight ECW bodies. Sixteen joined the fleet between 1977 and 1981.

buyer, but the Fleetline was also the standard double-decker at the West Midlands PTE. This reflected the fact that it had originally been produced in Coventry and that the PTE had followed the lead given by its constituent fleets in supporting a local manufacturer.

The last Fleetlines for West Midlands entered service in 1979 and were T-registered. Although a few survive, the type should have disappeared from the operations of WMPTE's privatised successor, West Midlands Travel, by the time this is in print — ousted by a remarkable influx of new Volvo single-deckers. The last WMPTE Fleetline was No 7000. Fleet No 7001 was the first of a new breed of double-decker on which Leyland was pinning its hopes — the Titan. Oh, well, they can't get it right all the time. To Leyland's chagrin, upstart integral manufacturer MCW stole West Midlands' business with its locally-produced Metrobus.

The Scottish Bus Group was another big Fleetline user, although from 1975 it was sharing its orders between the Fleetline and the Ailsa. The Ailsa's plus point was its simple layout and high passenger capacity. For SBG its big drawback was its height. SBG had long favoured lowbridge and lowheight double-deckers. Many of its buses would never actually encounter a

route with a low bridge, but by having an all lowheight/lowbridge fleet the group did have maximum flexibility in the allocation and use of its vehicles. The logic was that if one double-decker could get under a given low bridge, all double-deckers could.

Final Fleetline deliveries to SBG companies were in 1980 when Western SMT got 20 with V registrations which were followed later in the year by a batch of 20 W-registered buses for Alexander (Midland). These were the last new Fleetlines north of the border and fittingly had Alexander bodies of a style favoured by SBG since its first orders for the type in 1965. They had been stylish buses in 1965 and they didn't look too bad 15 years later, although as the 1980s wore on, their small windows and domed roofs did set them apart from other modern types. No Fleetlines survive in what were SBG fleets.

The last Fleetline chassis built went to South Notts and had lowheight ECW bodies, generally similar to those built for SBG. They entered service in 1981. Earlier chassis built for Cleveland Transit were bodied by Northern Counties and trickled out in small numbers up to 1983.

The fall in Fleetline deliveries was dramatic. In 1978 a total of 638 entered service in Britain. This figure was more than halved to 318 in 1979, then fell to 168 in 1980, 36 in 1981 and just six in 1982 before the last two took to the road in 1983.

When Fleetline production came to a close some 10,300 had been sold to British operators over a 21-year period. This compared with around 11,500 Atlanteans

over some 24 years. Indeed from 1967 to 1978 the Fleetline actually outsold the Atlantean in every year except 1969. The phasing out of the Fleetline at the end of the decade didn't immediately put the Atlantean in the lead (in 1980 more Bristol VRTs were sold than Atlanteans) and it was only in 1981 that the Atlantean once again became Britain's top-selling double-decker — which comes as a bit of a surprise in view of its widespread popularity with many major urban fleets.

By then, of course, the Atlantean itself was on the way out and in 1982 it was back in second place behind the new Olympian which was to replace it.

In the latter half of the 1970s around 600 Atlanteans a year were being put into service in Britain. This figure shot up to 660 in 1981 — the highest annual total in the model's long and illustrious history — before dropping dramatically to under 300 in 1982, then to 144 in 1983 and 134 in 1984.

During the 1970s the Atlantean had generally been a city operators' bus. It was never bought new by SBG, and it came a poor second to the Bristol VRT in NBC's orders. In most years NBC did not order any Atlanteans, but it did take occasional (and sizeable) batches. Its final Atlanteans were W-registered buses delivered in 1980/1 to Northern General (40)

Above:
London Transport became the world's biggest Daimler operator with its Fleetline fleet. All were withdrawn and sold prematurely, in the days when money could be squandered. A small number survive in service with other operators.

Below:
The Leyland Titan was conceived as a replacement for Leyland's ageing range of double-deck chassis. London Transport was the only significant buyer. An early Park Royal-built bus loads in East London. Many of London's Titans — perceived as unnecessarily complex when they were new — have enjoyed second lives with provincial fleets.

and London Country (56). These were bodied by Roe, to a design originally built by Park Royal for London Country but supplied during the 1970s to a number of NBC subsidiaries including East Yorkshire, Ribble, Southdown and Yorkshire Woollen. NBC also bought ECW-bodied Atlanteans.

However, it was to the PTEs that the Atlantean owed the bulk of its sales in the late 1970s. The last 100 for Glasgow — which actually turned out to be 99 plus an Olympian — were delivered in 1980/1 to the Strathclyde PTE and included eight X-registered buses. They brought to 1,448 the number of Atlanteans bought by the PTE and its predecessor, Glasgow Corporation. Many remain in all-day service in the city, but FirstBus, the present owners of Strathclyde Buses, is committed to fleet renewal and it is open to question whether Atlanteans will manage to clock up 40 years of unbroken service to Glaswegian travellers — the first entered service in 1958.

In Edinburgh, too, the Atlantean was the standard choice. Lothian's last batch, of 45 X-registered buses, entered service in 1981. With Lothian's legendary high-standards of care they look set to reach the millennium — which Edinburgh bus users might view as a mixed blessing in the days of air-sprung Olympians with low-emission Euro 2 engines.

Above:
The Tyne & Wear PTE was unusual in standardising on long-wheelbase AN68/2 Atlanteans. The last 30 were delivered in 1980/1 and like most of the Atlanteans bought by the PTE had Alexander bodies with panoramic windows. A substantial number remain in operation under Stagecoach ownership.

Above right:
Among the NBC fleets which bought Atlanteans was Northern General. The last, in 1980, had Roe bodies. A number survive.

Right:
Colchester bought Atlanteans with ECW bodies in the 1970s, a relatively unusual combination outside NBC fleets. Two climb North Hill on the approach to the town centre.

The two PTEs in the northwest of England were in the main Atlantean users and their Leyland legacy lives on in the streets of Liverpool and Manchester. Merseyside did buy Bristol VRTs and MCW Metropolitans, but for most of the 1970s the Atlantean was the fleet standard. Merseyside's final order, for 70, was delivered in 1983/4 and the very last was one of just four Atlanteans to enter service with B-prefix registrations (the only others were two for Blackpool and one for Fylde). The Atlantean was the only bus type of which examples could be seen

Above:
Former SBG Leopards have been popular second-hand buys with all types of operators. New to Western SMT in 1974, this bus reached Lincolnshire RoadCar in 1989. It was previously owned by Gash of Newark.

with both 1964 B-suffix registrations and 1984 B-prefix numbers, although in fairness to Leyland, the model had been developed over the years and the last AN68 was a rather different beast from the original PDR1.

Merseyside's Atlanteans have proved particularly durable and until recently 20-year-old AN68s could be seen on all-day service. The mid-1990s have seen a steady influx of new buses to Merseyside Transport, the PTE's successor, and a consequent reduction in the Atlantean fleet. Their days may be numbered, but the final countdown looks to be still a little way off.

In Greater Manchester the PTE bought both Fleetlines and Atlanteans. There were 500 standard Fleetlines, delivered between 1972 and 1980, and 1,265 standard Atlanteans, spanning the years from 1972 to 1984. There should in fact have been 1,325, but the last 60 were cancelled and Olympians ordered in their place.

Of the Greater Manchester Atlanteans, some 500 entered service between 1980 and 1984 and a fair number of these remain in service with the two companies which have succeeded the PTE. Greater

Manchester Buses North, now part of FirstBus, inherited over 400 Atlanteans when it was privatised in 1994, while Greater Manchester Buses South, now a Stagecoach subsidiary, took just under 300. Both FirstBus and Stagecoach have injected large numbers of new buses into their Manchester fleets. The Fleetline has gone from GM Buses South and is disappearing at GM Buses North; the Atlantean is following it. But not, as these words are written, at breakneck speed.

The two Yorkshire PTEs both ran Atlanteans. West Yorkshire added 361 to its fleet between 1974 and 1981, all with bodies built in Leeds by Roe. This compares with 156 Fleetlines in the period 1976-8. The PTE's bus operations are now in the hands of Yorkshire Rider, part of FirstBus, and Atlanteans are still in operation in decreasing numbers. The Fleetlines have all been withdrawn.

The South Yorkshire PTE was less enamoured of Leyland's products, as witnessed by the delivery of 62 Ailsas in 1976/7, and the fleet's switch to the Dennis Dominator from 1981. The PTE did buy both Fleetlines and Atlanteans, with the former including a batch of DMS look-alikes in 1977 before its final batch of S-registered Alexander-bodied buses in 1978.

Leyland's preparedness (willingness might be putting it too strongly) to fit Voith gearboxes to Atlanteans helped secure ongoing Atlantean orders and the model did quite well towards the end — 236 were supplied between 1978 and 1981 when the last W-registered

Above:
The standard NBC bus for most of the 1970s was the Bristol VRT with lowheight ECW bodywork. This Southdown bus in Southsea was not quite typical of the breed, having been built with two doors. By 1991 the centre exit had been removed, but the centrally-positioned staircase remains as a clue to its original layout.

AN68s took to South Yorkshire's streets. These were doubly unusual in that not only did they have Voith gearboxes, but they had double-deck Marshall bodies. SYPTE's insistence on Voith gearboxes in preference to the standard Leyland Pneumocyclic was on account of the German gearbox having a retarder, which helped reduce brake lining wear on Sheffield's hilly routes. Other Leyland buyers had to wait for the appearance of the Hydracyclic in the Titan and Olympian to get the benefits of a retarder.

All of South Yorkshire's Atlanteans have gone, and the oldest buses now in operation are the vanguard of the next generation of rear-engined 'deckers, MCW Metrobuses.

And so to the Bristol VRT. When the first VRTs entered service in 1968 the Atlantean had been around for 10 years and the Fleetline for eight. Initial orders came mainly from Tilling group companies and then from the newly-formed NBC which came into being at the start of 1969. SBG tried it and didn't like it, and VRT orders were also placed by Liverpool Corporation, the Merseyside and West Midlands PTEs and, as the 1970s wore on, by a growing number of municipal fleets including Cardiff, Lincoln, Northampton and Tayside Region. Tayside didn't like them either, and by the early 1980s out of 134 VRTs delivered new to Scottish fleets the only one left was a Tayside open-topper. VRTs were often ordered as substitutes for Fleetlines which were in short supply because of London orders and the

disruption caused by the transfer of production from Coventry to Leyland.

Fortunately for Bristol, the VRT did rather better south of the border and it became the standard NBC double-decker. In round figures, of almost 4,500 built, some 3,750 — 84% — were for Tilling/NBC fleets. Orders were slow in coming in the early 1970s. By 1972 there were just 650 in operation, representing five years' deliveries — a figure which was less than one year's sales of Fleetlines in Britain. But the numbers steadily rose — new deliveries totalled 342 in 1975, 400 in 1976 and 532 in 1977 to reach a peak of 632 in 1980, which made the VRT Britain's best-selling double-decker in that year, ahead of the Fleetline and the Atlantean.

The last VRTs carried X-suffix registrations. X-registered VRTs were delivered to NBC subsidiaries Crosville, East Kent, East Yorkshire, Eastern Counties, Eastern National, Trent, United Auto, West Riding and Yorkshire Traction. Such have been the changes among NBC companies both before and after privatisation that many of the vehicles which it owned have been scattered far and wide. But substantial fleets of VRTs survive across the country, and the VRT enjoys a relatively high survival rate. The last VRT to leave the ECW factory at Lowestoft went to Eastern Counties in the autumn of 1981.

However, if you apply the good old 15-year-life rule, then all should be gone, so it's not unreasonable to see the VRT as just as much a threatened species as the more numerous Atlanteans and Fleetlines which were its contemporaries.

The most successful of Leyland's mid-1970 competitors was the Ailsa, built in Scotland and operated in reasonable numbers by SBG, Greater Glasgow, Tayside, West Midlands and South Yorkshire. The Ailsa peaked early, with 148 being put into service in 1976, a figure which must have heartened the Ailsa sales team just as much as the meagre 50 delivered in the following year must have disheartened them. Sales in the late 1970s averaged just over 50 a year. Ailsa production continued until 1984, when the mid-engined Volvo Citybus, developed from the B10M coach chassis, replaced it. Ailsas were never widespread and now are to be found principally in Glasgow, Dundee and Leeds where Black Prince has built up a fleet of second-hand examples. Although the model was developed at the behest of the Scottish Bus Group, few survive with erstwhile SBG users. The remaining users are Fife Scottish and SMT.

The reason that so many double-deck types are vanishing has a lot to do with the timing of model launches by Leyland whose share of the double-deck market in the late 1970s peaked at 95.8% in 1978, after having been 100% — these figures include Bristol, part owned by British Leyland — before the arrival of the Ailsa and the short-lived Metropolitan from MCW. (This figure plummeted to 68.9% in 1980, a position from which Leyland would never regain its former pre-eminence.) Despite the best efforts of MCW, Foden (remember them?) and Ailsa in the mid-1970s, Leyland still ruled the roost. So it was Leyland's plans which dictated most of what was happening to double-deckers, and what it wanted was rationalisation. Why build three models when one would do, as the Leyland National had — more or less — demonstrated?

The Titan made its first faltering appearance in 1977, limped into 1978 and died in 1984 after just 1,158 had been built. (Compare that with Fleetline deliveries of 1,129 in 1973 alone.)

The Olympian followed in 1981 — which means early W- and X-registered Olympians are now due for withdrawal — and the fates of the Fleetline, VRT and Atlantean were sealed.

The single-deck story is rather different. The Leyland National was launched in 1972 and the oldest examples are now well past their use-by date. The models which the National replaced — AEC Swift, Leyland Panther and Bristol RE — have almost all been consigned to the scrap-heap.

Right:
The Leyland Leopard with Alexander Y-type body first entered Scottish Bus Group service in 1963. The Y-type's designer could not have foreseen that over 30 years later the model would still be commonplace in Scotland. A 1977 Leopard in the Western Scottish fleet roars in to Paisley in 1991.

Below:
Atlanteans featured prominently in municipal fleets and nowhere more so than in Lancashire, Leyland's home territory. Preston standardised on long-wheelbase AN68/2s. Most were built as two-door buses, but this is one of a pair which had single-doorway East Lancs coach bodies.

Left:
Atlanteans have played a major part in transporting the citizens of Greater Manchester for a quarter of a century, but are now on the way out. This late AN68 with Northern Counties body is negotiating work in connection with the Metrolink system in 1991. It was one of almost 300 Atlanteans to be inherited by GM Buses South when the PTE-owned company was privatised.

Below:
Blackburn's last Atlanteans entered service in 1983 and, like most of the fleet, had bodies built in the town by East Lancs. They remain the operator's most modern double-deckers — all subsequent purchases have been single-deckers or small buses.

UK sales of the National peaked in 1978 at 939. This was followed by the launch of the initially troublesome National 2, and after 1981 annual sales of the National never reached treble figures; which posed a bit of a problem for a factory designed to build 2,000 buses a year. As a result, National 2s are relatively rare when compared with National 1s, as the original model almost inevitably came to be retrospectively known. But the durability of the National structure is such that it would be a braver man than I who would forecast the imminent disappearance of Nationals from Britain's roads, however desirable a thing that might be.

The other common model which ought to be a threatened species is Leyland's Leopard. The Leopard has a long and honourable history, from the launch of the original 30ft-long L1 and L2 models in 1959, through the later PSU3, PSU4 and PSU5 variants. The PSU3 became popular as a bus with SBG companies, which avoided (with some justification) the low-frame rear-engined designs on offer in the 1960s.

Ease of access, although not the high-profile issue it has become in the 1990s, was a concern in the 1960s and early rear-engined double-deckers did offer a step-free entrance. Leyland, indeed, had coined the term 'Low-loader' for the precursors of what became the Atlantean. But in Scotland the Scottish Bus Group workhorse was the 36ft-long PSU3/3 Leopard with manual gearbox and Alexander Y-type body. The first Y-type Leopards entered service with Western SMT in 1963. The last were delivered in 1982 to Fife, Midland and Central, which between them received 26 Y-registered Y-types.

Redundant SBG Y-type Leopards found ready buyers

among post-deregulation independents as a number of SBG companies were forced to cut back their operations in the late 1980s. But Y-type Leopards still roam the streets of a good number of Scottish towns (as do Seddon Pennines with Y-type bodies, another combination favoured by SBG until 1982). Leopards remain in a number of what were SBG fleets, including Bluebird Buses, Clydeside, Fife Scottish, Highland Country, Midland Bluebird and Western Buses. They may be simple. They may be reliable. They may be economical. But they are not buses for the future. Watch out — they'll soon be gone.

Elsewhere the same fate faces the Leopard, with the distinctive throaty growl of the Leyland 680 engine

(somehow the TL11-powered Tiger seemed tamer). Leopard buses have gone from the Greater Manchester fleet, after many years of service in the Bolton and Leigh areas. They've gone from Yorkshire Rider, where they were long a familiar sight in Halifax. They survive with some smaller operators like Burnley & Pendle (although surely not for much longer now that Stagecoach is in control), Islwyn Borough Transport and, of course, with the myriad of independents who are prepared to live with the Leopard's vices in order to benefit from its virtues. The Leopard's great contemporary, the AEC Reliance, is also only to be found with small independents — and since latterly most Reliances were coaches, you'll look long and hard to find a Reliance on

Above:
The last Fleetlines for the West Midlands PTE entered service in 1979 and had 76-seat MCW bodies. One of the final batch is seen in Coventry in the late 1980s.

Left:
The integral Leyland National — a joint Leyland/NBC project — depended to a large extent on NBC orders. A number of NBC fleets specified coach seats in Nationals, including Crosville with this 11.6m dual-purpose vehicle seen in Liverpool. The National structure has proved to be long-lived.

a bus route.

At the risk of stating the obvious, change has always been with us (except for travellers on farebox-equipped Lothian Region buses). Did anyone lament the withdrawal of the last Leyland Leviathan in the 1930s? Or of the last TD1 Titan? Or the last wartime Guy? I'm sure they didn't. Like the Atlanteans, Fleetlines and VRTs which are daily disappearing from our streets, they passed unnoticed. All I'm saying is enjoy them — or if you're a user, endure them — while you can. Tomorrow may be too late.

Left:
Merseyside PTE's Atlanteans were to prove remarkably long-lived, many lasting for 20 years. A 1973 AN68 with East Lancs body sweeps into the Pier Head bus station in Liverpool in 1986.

Right:
SBG wanted Gardner-engined single-deckers in the 1970s, and Seddon built them. An Eastern Scottish Pennine VII with Alexander body leaves Glasgow's Buchanan bus station. The 1982 X-registered batch was the last — and marked the end of bus production by Seddon.

Below:
Scotland's last Fleetlines were delivered in 1980 to Alexander (Midland). They had Alexander bodies which looked little different from those on the first SBG Fleetlines in 1965. One is seen in Falkirk when new.

The Bristol name is inextricably linked with state-owned bus operators. **Kevin Lane** illustrates a selection of Bristols which have seen service with local authority fleets

Top:
In the late 1940s a few municipal fleets bought Bristol Ks and Ls before the Bristol factory passed into state ownership. This AEC-engined K6A with Roe body was one of four delivered to Doncaster Corporation in 1947/8. Doncaster had bought Bristols in the 1930s. Kevin Lane collection

Above:
A much later municipal Bristol is this 1969 ECW-bodied RELL in the Luton Corporation fleet. Luton had in 1967 started moving from double-deck to single-deck operation, and when it sold its bus fleet to United Counties at the start of 1970 had 30 of these RELL6Ls. Kevin Lane collection

Top:
Leicester Corporation also bought REs between 1967 and 1970, before switching its orders to the new Metro-Scania in 1971. There were 28, all with ECW bodies and Leyland engines. Kevin Lane

Above;
The SELNEC Passenger Transport Executive operated a variety of Bristols, including six short-wheelbase RESL6Gs with unusual 43-seat Northern Counties bodies. These had been new to the Stalybridge, Hyde, Mossley and Dukinfield joint board. Kevin Lane

Above:
Cardiff Corporation was a major Bristol user, running VRTs with bodies by Alexander, Willowbrook and, as seen here, ECW. This bus is seen in the livery of the Tyne & Wear PTE, to whom it was hired in 1978-79. Kevin Lane

Below:
A Cardiff Bristol on home ground in 1990. This is a VRT with Alexander body, one of 71 delivered in 1979-80. Kevin Lane

Top:
The West Midlands PTE bought 200 VRTs which were bodied in Birmingham by Metro-Cammell and looked broadly similar to contemporary Daimler Fleetlines, apart from the grille in the front panel which provided a flow of air to the VRT's front-mounted radiator. This VRT is seen in Sutton Coldfield in 1982. *Kevin Lane*

Above:
Most of the Merseyside PTE's double-deckers were Atlanteans, but it did run 109 VRTs with East Lancs bodywork. This is a long-wheelbase VRT/LH which was one of 59 delivered in 1970-71. They had been ordered by Liverpool Corporation.
Kevin Lane collection

Above left:
The lightweight Bristol LH was popular with a number of NBC fleets, but was also bought by London Transport. In the early 1980s Thamesdown Transport was running six ex-London LHs of which two, including this 1976 bus, had come via Davies of Carmarthen. It is seen in Marlborough. Kevin Lane collection

Left:
The early days of deregulation saw some unusual vehicle movements. An East Kent LH, complete with NBC logo on the grille, is seen running on hire to Boro'line, the trading name adopted by Maidstone Borough Transport in 1986. Kevin Lane

Above:
Second-hand Bristol REs proved popular with Busways, the former Tyne & Wear PTE operation, in the mid 1980s. This ECW-bodied bus had been new to the Merseyside PTE and is seen in South Shields in September 1986. Kevin Lane

Right:
To tackle post-deregulation competition established operators often found themselves running unusual types, as demonstrated by a Bristol VRT in the colours of Bournemouth Transport. The bus had been new to Yorkshire Traction and is seen in Bournemouth in 1994. Kevin Lane

NORTH FROM ENFIELD

When local bus services were deregulated in 1986 London Buses started to compete with London Country North East between Enfield and Hertford. **Simon Butler** illustrates a selection of vehicles used.

Left:
Routemasters have appeared on the service on just two occasions. This 1964 bus is seen in Hoddesdon in September 1989 on the occasion of a railway exhibition.
ALL PHOTOGRAPHS BY THE AUTHOR

Below:
Potters Bar operated ex-South Yorkshire Ailsas with striking bodies by Van Hool-McArdle and these, too, could be seen on the 310A.

Left:
The mainstay of London Buses' Route 310A from Enfield to Hertford from the start was the MCW Metrobus. A southbound example passes through Waltham Cross in January 1987.

Right:
Alexander bodywork was fitted to a batch of ex-West Yorkshire MCW Metrobuses. The Alexander/MCW combination was rare outside Scotland.

Left:
London Buses bought 50 Alexander-bodied Ailsas from West Midlands, and some of these were used regularly on the 310A from Potters Bar garage. In this 1989 view London Northern fleetnames are carried — marking an early stage in the break-up and eventual privatisation of London Buses.

Top left:
The three Ailsas bought new by London Buses eventually found their way to Potters Bar. They had Alexander R-type bodies. One loads at Hoddesdon Clock in 1987.

Left:
The route is now operated by MTL London using single-deckers. This DAF SB220 with Ikarus bodywork was new to Ogden of St Helens and was photographed in Hertford in August 1996. Note the three-track number blind with the 'A' being featured on the main destination screen.

Below:
Also acquired from Ogden of St Helens following their withdrawal from local bus operation was this Optare-bodied DAF, seen heading through Waltham Cross on its way to Hertford. It, too, features a cleverly-adapted display to show route number 310B.

WHICH WAY FORWARD?

Michael H. C. Baker reflects on the strengths and weaknesses of public transport during a recent safari in northwest England.

Above:
A Merseybus Alexander-bodied Atlantean of 1983 leads a line of double-deckers in Liverpool.
ALL PHOTOGRAPHS BY THE AUTHOR

Few citizens nowadays argue against the need for better public transport, the myth that deregulation would bring this about has been exploded, and here and there things really are getting better. But overall I cannot see any great cause for rejoicing, yet. Living in a small rural town and having to make a 10-mile journey to work I almost invariably travel by car, usually sharing transport with a colleague. There is an hourly bus service but the times don't fit in the morning and the time I leave for home varies each evening. Nevertheless, I do occasionally use the bus, which stops outside the school where I teach and at the other end at several places on my own road. 'Catching the bus; surely there's someone who can give you a lift?' is the usual astonished response. Travelling by bus is seen as a very odd thing to

do: eccentric and outside most people's normal experience.

This seems to me almost the greatest obstacle to overcome if bus, or perhaps tram, travel is to regain its position in mainstream society. Fifty years ago when I started going to school vastly fewer families had cars than now — we did, but it was only used for weekend outings and holidays and was sold when my twin sisters arrived; we couldn't afford both, or rather all three —

Above;
Twenty years separate the Merseybus Atlantean from the Liverbus Volvo B10B, seen in central Liverpool.

and everyone I knew went to school and work by bus, tram or train. Then I lived in the London suburbs, where public transport was vastly more accessible but when I visited relations in the country they too relied on what public transport there was — and their bicycles.

While traffic congestion has increased enormously in the suburbs, although less so in the city and town centres where, thankfully, pedestrianisation and bus and tram priority have become more commonplace, the rural areas have suffered to a greater extent than the urban ones as more and more families and individuals have acquired cars. Certainly this is so in those areas I've lived in: the Surrey/Sussex/Kent border regions, Dorset, the Welsh Marches and Lancashire. First the two-man or -woman double-decker disappeared, then the full-size single-deckers became less frequent, later still they were often replaced by minibuses or have disappeared altogether. And where they are still used, no longer does one find a cross-section of the community amongst the passengers. School children, mothers with toddlers, and the elderly make up the majority. In other words, the less well off.

Whilst to be without a car would be highly inconvenient, the pendulum has swung too far towards accommodating it and one would like to see steps taken to actively encourage much greater use by all sections of the community, in both towns and countryside, of public transport. I recently spent several days travelling in Lancashire, partly in familiar haunts, partly in unfamiliar ones; I enjoyed myself, but whether I found cause for

optimism is difficult to say. I leave the reader to draw his or her own conclusions.

In the 1950s and 1960s I lived on Merseyside, on both sides of the river, and my first journey last autumn was from the St John's bus station, then being rebuilt, in Liverpool, to Birkenhead. In all the journeys I made over or under the Mersey, I'd never before travelled by scheduled bus. At one time only night services ran through the tunnel, but with the opening of the second Wallasey Tunnel in 1971, regular daily ones began, operated by the PTE and later also by Crosville. For generations services in and out of Liverpool city centre used to be based on the Pier Head, but with the decline of the ferries which now operate in the morning and evening peak for a band of dedicated commuters but otherwise only as a tourist attraction — better that than disappearing completely — use of this terminus has declined drastically. Most passengers not in cars cross by Merseyrail electric trains, but a whole raft of bus routes also links Liverpool with the Wirral.

Merseyrider, successor of Liverpool Corporation, Merseyside PTE and now part of the MTL empire and generally known as Merseybus, was operating in a

variety of liveries, one being London red for it had a large fleet of Titans bought from the capital, many of which it had not yet got around to repainting, more than two years later. Liverpool buses were seldom renowned for their luxurious appointments, although the huge fleet of purpose-built MCW Atlanteans, the first of which entered service in February 1963 on my local routes, 86/7, were fine vehicles and honourable exceptions. At the time of my trip the Merseybus fleet was distinctly elderly, the newest double-deckers in Merseybus livery being a batch of Alexander-bodied Olympians delivered in 1989. Recent deliveries were single-deckers, including the first ultra-low floor ones to enter service in the UK, five Neoplan N4014s turned out in grey, yellow and white SMART livery, which operated a contracted route from Aigburth to the Albert Dock and were therefore much in the eye of tourists.

However, inhabiting a shadowy existence somewhere between native and visitor, I was provided with a venerable Alexander-bodied AN68 Atlantean built in 1972. Merseybus still relies heavily on Atlanteans dating from the 1970s, many with distinctive peaks at the front and rear domes, a feature introduced on the 1963 Atlanteans. The graffiti on the upper deck was relatively unobtrusive as were the rattles, not bad for a double-decker which had spent 23 years pounding the streets of Liverpool, and with a respectable load aboard. After negotiating the big-dipper-like approach to the tunnel we sped through it in fine style, passing another Atlantean as the light at the end of the tunnel approached.

The previous year I had seen a revival of the old blue and cream Birkenhead Corporation livery on the Greater Manchester Buses South which had opened up at a depot in the town — there had also been standard orange, brown and white-liveried GM buses in Liverpool — but these had retreated leaving Merseybus in charge of the majority of Birkenhead and Wallasey services. I had

thought that Birkenhead docks, like so much of the Merseyside dock system, had closed completely to commercial traffic but I found a large freighter from the Far East loading, opposite an elderly laid-up Isle of Man ferry, as maroon and cream Atlanteans dashed across a swingbridge separating them.

Unlike the Pier Head at Liverpool, Birkenhead Woodside remains the principal terminus for both local and long-distance bus services, and the Crosville fleetname is still a familiar sight there occupying with Merseybus the handsome new terminus. When I first knew Woodside, large numbers of regular passengers still used the ferries and it was possible to walk straight off them onto a steam train which would take one all the

where a number of trams from Birkenhead and Liverpool, either under restoration or completed, are housed along with buses, including a Routemaster restored to London livery and which regularly operates special services.

I was to travel on trams of a very different type several times in the next few days for we were staying in a cottage up in the Pennines above Ramsbottom; we had business in Manchester and far and away the most comfortable and trouble-free method of getting there was to drive to Bury and take the Metrolink into the city centre. Our business one evening consisted of going to the pictures near Albert Square. We emerged from the cinema just in time to see a tram drawing up; we dashed across and boarded it, riding in comfort through the heart of the city, the traffic lights programmed to give priority to the tram. At Victoria station we took to railway tracks and bowled along in fine style through the northern suburbs until we reached the Bury terminus. To be able to board a public service vehicle in the heart of a city which makes use of the street pattern and once beyond them travels at railway speeds, enabling one to abandon all worries about car parking and ride home relaxed and in comfort, is surely an ideal to which all travellers in large conurbations ought to be able to aspire as the 20th century comes to an end. Whilst trams are perhaps the ideal, well-sprung and well-insulated buses capable of speeds up to 70mph and given priority will do just as well.

My next journey fell somewhat short of these lofty notions. I had taken the train from Manchester to Wigan, using a Wayfarer ticket which cost £5.20 for the day and enabled one to travel as far south of Manchester as Buxton and Macclesfield, east to Glossop, north to Rochdale and Darwen and west to Warrington and Wigan by practically any train or bus, though not, for some daft reasoning, on the trams either to Bury or Altrincham. Otherwise great value. It even entitled you to free admittance to the Manchester Museum of Transport with its wonderful collection of vintage buses, coaches and trolleybuses.

Wigan used to boast some of the handsomest buses in Lancashire: Leylands with Leyland- or Wigan-built

way to Paddington. The railway has gone but the area remains a fascinating one for the transport enthusiast for there is a restored horse tram dating from 1876 in the ferry terminus, and, even better, it is possible to actually ride on a tram to a museum where more trams and buses are being restored and on display.

It is perhaps carping to quibble with the description of the two double-deck trams which regularly operate the service from Woodside as 'approximate to the type common on the streets of Britain in the forties and fifties' which is what the brochure put out by EuroWirral (my!) and the Metropolitan Borough claims, for it also informs us they were built in Hong Kong in 1992 to a 1948 pattern with wooden, low-back seats, which actually makes them a good deal more primitive than contemporary British trams. The last Birkenhead Corporation tram was taken out of service in 1937, but I knew Liverpool trams well — they didn't disappear for another 20 years, and they were very comfortable vehicles. However, it's a fine thing to find trams of any description running again in Birkenhead and I was conveyed to the Pacific Road Large Objects Museum

Massey bodies painted in a fine and dignified maroon and white livery with shaded gold numbers. The corporation got swallowed up, for not entirely obvious reasons, by the Greater Manchester PTE, but that was long ago and today GM Buses North has taken their place, many of its buses having Wigan-built Northern Counties bodies. North Western, the successor of Ribble, also maintains a presence in the town, as does Merseybus, whilst there are a number of smaller operators.

Resisting the siren calls of Wigan Pier, I looked for a bus to take me to Bolton and boarded a Blue Bus (not to be confused with Blue Buses of Lytham St Annes) single-decker. This was a very second-hand Alexander-bodied Leyland Leopard. Blue Bus, based in Horwich, owns around 30 vehicles, most of them elderly Leopards and Atlanteans it has acquired from various sources.

'Oh, shurrup!' growled the driver to another who was vigorously hooting us to get out of his way. We left with a respectable cargo of 28 souls, mostly elderly shoppers.

The seats were upholstered in a remarkable variety of patterns and colours. I sat with my knees up around my neck admiring the unique plastic wood veneer of the seat in front, moved to the very back where there was more leg-room but the propensity for travel sickness was much higher and eventually, as various pensioners disembarked, made myself as comfortable as I could with my legs stuck out in the gangway. The driver, attired more for a Sunday afternoon snooze in front of the telly than command of an interurban PSV, proved to be a friendly soul, chatting to many of the passengers who were obviously regulars; one or two even seemingly just waiting to pass the time of day at the stop without actually climbing aboard. We took many diversions in and out of housing estates, typical of such services, worming our way between parked T-reg Nissans and elderly Sierras with multicoloured doors, and whenever we speeded up the windows rattled as though to shake themselves out of their frames. A placard outside a local newsagent announcing 'Bolton woman to see hypnotist' and then the sight of a large shed with a sign above it: 'Bolton Olympic Wrestling Club' heralded our destination.

Bolton bus station is always a hive of activity, GM Buses North and Ribble dominate with examples of practically every type of vehicle in their large fleets,

Below:
The Blue Bus fleet contains a large number of Leyland Leopards. The Alexander Y-type body on this bus unloading in Bolton has had a deeper destination display fitted.

Above:
GM Buses North has invested in high-quality new buses, such as this Volvo B10B with Wright bodywork. Two Ribble Nationals load behind.

from minibuses, through the rare GM Lynx — and there are only four, all natives of Bolton — to brand-new single-deckers and various double-deck buses and coaches. I bought a large mug of tea in the café for 30p, terrific value, and then joined the queue for the X25. This is a Ribble service which runs hourly from Manchester to Clitheroe. The queue was lengthy and our coach when it pulled in 5min late was already pretty full. However, a large number got out, leaving just about enough room for the large number that got in. We had a young driver and an inspector and we were all of 10min late when we pulled out and headed north.

Ribble was, of course, one of the great pioneers of both long- and short-distance express services and I can remember the stir caused by the double-deck White Lady PD1s and PD2s of the early postwar years which operated all over Lancashire and beyond. Our vehicle, a Leyland Tiger of 1985 with a Duple Laser body, was rather less exotic but nevertheless very comfortable, particularly in comparison with the Blue Bus Leopard. High-back coach seats make a great deal of difference to the ambience of a PSV. I've avoided travel in Leyland Nationals whenever possible, not least because of their miserable seats. I was waiting at Ramsbottom a couple of days later for a 273, expecting one of the new Plaxton Premiere Interurban-bodied Dennis Javelins and was much put out when an elderly Ribble National rolled up. However, its high-backed seating was a surprise and made the journey much more pleasant.

To return to the X25. The clientele was rather more varied than on the Wigan-Bolton service, with a greater air of affluence. It was roadworks season in north Bolton but we eventually cleared them and now the scenery was quite different to anything I had so far encountered. Industry, old and new, grand public buildings, mean terraces and handsome semi-detacheds were left behind as we headed out on the moorland slopes of the west Pennines. We climbed to the heights of Entwistle, past grey stone farms and then swept down towards Darwen, its approach signalled by a tall, ornate mill chimney towering above the town. I alighted by the town hall, read one of those local paper headlines that almost makes you buy the paper: 'Darwen chef linked with Mafia', but dragged myself away to concentrate on the serious business of watching the comings and goings at the bus station where various Blackburn Transport buses drew up, not least East Lancashire Greenways. Being a local project, Blackburn has taken a great interest in these revamped Nationals and bought its first in 1993. I watched the next southbound X25 depart, a slightly older Duple-bodied Tiger, a Dominant IV of 1983, and then headed up the hill to the railway station to catch a Sprinter back to Bolton.

I couldn't resist another 30p mug of tea, and then looked around for a conveyance back to Manchester. There's never any shortage of these in Bolton and I could have waited for the next X25. However, the very next service out was a GM Buses North No 8 and being a double-decker with the pole position upstairs front vacant where I could pretend I was driving and go 'brmm brmm' to my heart's content, I leaped aboard. The bus was a Manchester Standard, a Northern Counties-bodied Atlantean of 1984, a perfectly decent vehicle, although not up to the coach seated pink-hued version I had sampled a day earlier, on the X86 from Rawtenstall to Ramsbottom. Pink sounds a very effete colour for a Lancashire double-decker but it actually looks rather good on Manchester buses, as long as it's kept clean.

Off we went past the Wanderers' ground, already at that stage of the season struggling to hold on to its newly-won Premier League position, past yet another arresting headline 'Fred Dibnah joins Bolton's Heritage Row' — I looked in vain to see of he was holding a sit-in on any of the surrounding mill chimneys which are still plentiful in these parts — and then studied the poster on the back of the bus in front.

'When a car hits a bus the car stops dead, when a bus hits a car the car accelerates! Please be careful.' Taking this to heart I sat bolt upright with my arms folded as we swept through sedate Kearsley, overtook a lady on horseback, and then the M62, and stopped to pick up another lady in a very short black miniskirt and large sunglasses, presumably donned to cope with the rather wan October sun which was now setting over Tyldesley.

We overtook the preceding bus beside a wonderful art deco cinema in Pendlebury, only for it to come sweeping past on the outside at Salford art gallery, home of the finest collection in the world of L. S. Lowry paintings, drawings and memorabilia. Here several students

Below:
Ribble uses smart long-wheelbase Olympians on its Manchester to Colne express. They have Alexander bodies with high-backed seats. A more basic Atlantean of GM Buses North is on the left.

boarded, the first passengers to join me upstairs since leaving Bolton. The lights were now coming on in the high-rise skyline ahead, very different to the Salford and Manchester which the great man painted, but not without its own appeal. With the Irwell on one side and the Coronation Street studios and the world's oldest railway station just down the road on the other, we headed past the Salford/Manchester boundary and the one-time terminus of dignified, poster-less, green Salford Corporation Metro-Cammell-bodied CV Daimlers, before drawing into the cavernous interior of the Arndale Centre bus station, a good 10min early.

So what to make of my Lancashire journeys? The double-decker has been part of the British scene almost since the beginning and in Lancashire, a particular stronghold, one only had to visit the Manchester Transport Museum to be reminded of this. I came across a few new M- and N-reg ones, in the Liverbus and Mayne fleets for instance, whilst Ribble remained faithful to its traditions with some fairly new Alexander-bodied long-wheelbase Olympians fitted with high-backed seats branded for the 'Mancunian Network 2000 Service'. There were new single-deckers aplenty, the ultra-lowfloor Merseybus ones, and North Western Dennis Falcons in Liverpool for example; whilst to quote then Managing Director Dr Alan Westwell of GM Buses North, 'We had a lot of vandalism on double-deckers, and unions and management agreed that we should go for large-capacity single-deckers'. Hence the Volvo B10Bs with Wright bodies and low, but not ultra-low, floors, marketed as Superbuses. Then, of course, there are the Metrolink trams. With their seating capacity of 86, huge standing capacity and double all this when two units work together as they do at rush-hours, then there is no way the double-deck bus can compete. Trams can last a very long time: quite recently I travelled in some PCC-type cars in Milan dating from the late 1920s which are still perfectly acceptable, but the bus is rather different. Poor seating and rattling

Above:
The top deck of a bus provides a novel vantage point for photography. This is Rawtenstall in 1995, with a 10-year-old Northern Counties-bodied Olympian of GM Buses North.

Right:
On the bleak West Pennine Moors between Darwen and Bolton, a Ribble Tiger with Duple Laser body heads south on the X25 express service.

windows are a severe turn-off and these, together with shabby, unco-ordinated interiors, give an air of downmarket third-rate travel reminiscent of the last days of steam railway compartment stock or Southern Electric EPBs.

I'm sure the double-decker does have a future, although a more restricted one. As I was completing this article, Neil Kinnock, the ECC Commissioner responsible for Transport, announced his consultative document which recommends that 90% of future funding should go on various forms of public transport. Whatever some citizens' views of Europe, this is surely the way forward for all its members.

Joy Ride

John Aldridge
takes a holiday bus trip.

We were on holiday, a day's outing away from our holiday base, in a town I had not visited for years. They — the rest of the family — were going round the shops, while I had sloped off to study the local bus scene. Some locations can be quite boring these days, particularly if there is just one major operator with a limited range of types. This town — name suppressed to protect the innocent — seemed such a place.

But then, at the far end of the road where the bus services started, I spotted an elderly something-or-other with an Alexander Y-type bus body, belonging to a small operator. I took a picture first, then walked round it, thinking no doubt it was a Leyland Leopard. But a glance through the (closed) doors revealed an engine cover and a strange entrance arrangement alongside it — a Ford. Its V registration made it a relatively late model, obviously ex-Scottish Bus Group, and also a relatively uncommon combination, as most full-sized Ford PSVs were bodied as coaches.

I waited for the driver to reappear, and had a brief chat. Not surprisingly, I gathered he did not think a lot of the vehicle.

A study of the timetable revealed it to be on a one-bus route with a round trip time of just under an hour. I went off, met up with the family who were in no hurry to leave, had a snack and then returned to the terminal to await the Ford's next appearance. It was lunchtime and there appeared to be only two other likely passengers. They were foreign tourists, one of whom asked the driver complicated questions, translated the answers to his companion and then argued with the driver about his answers.

'Either you want this bus, or you don't, and I haven't got all day to hang about,' said the driver, revving the engine. Reluctantly the tourist got off, the doors shut and we were away.

The interior was in good order and clean, the seat moquette still bright, and the general ambience was good: Y-type interiors wear well and still look modern. The driver too was smart, probably in his late 50s, with grey hair, short-sleeved blue shirt and blue trousers neatly pressed.

After negotiating one-way streets and tight roundabouts we climbed steeply out of town. With an almost empty bus the noise was formidable. The doors, the ticket machine bracket, the windows, the interior cab door and the seats all vibrated continuously, doing their unsuccessful best to drown the sound of the worn Ford engine. Still on the gradient there was a T-junction, at which we stopped and then made a sharp right turn, still climbing. The driver handled the gearbox well; not easy on a Ford. Level, high, ground was reached and soon we darted off to the right by a sign reading 'No through road' into a housing estate. We drove almost to the end of the estate, backed into a kind of turning area and retraced our steps to the original turn-off, having neither set down nor picked up any passengers.

It was obviously a quiet journey (in passenger, not mechanical, terms) and — knowing I was an enthusiast — the driver was quite chatty.

'Did you hear the din when we climbed out of town?' he asked, continuing: 'A day on this bus and I go home with a head "out here" and a permanent headache.'

The road narrowed, with just the occasional wider section, the odd cluster of houses, and even a brick-built bus shelter. The driver returned to his theme. 'He doesn't give me this one to drive very often. He knows what I think about it. He waits till he thinks I've forgotten what it was like last time, and then gives it to me again.'

The road narrowed to little more than bus width, and the occasional cars we encountered gave way, or even backed to let us through. We drove through carefully, but imperiously, not thanking any of them. Next came a strange, rural crossroads, with a 'No entry' sign ahead. We dived left into another single-lane road and soon reached the terminus, which was obstructed by a row of parked cars. The driver remarked on the selfishness of car drivers. I got out and took a photo.

'It's amazing,' he said as I rejoined. 'I'm paid to drive this thing. You're actually voluntarily paying good money to ride on it. He only bought it because it was cheap, you know; the rest of the fleet's far nicer.'

Off we went down fresh narrow roads, before rejoining our old route from the other direction along the 'No entry' road I'd noticed earlier. We turned sharp left, and stopped to pick up a couple of passengers, with whom the driver exchanged pleasantries. Then came another narrow section. I asked if he would mind stopping for me to take a picture. No problem. I got back on. 'When you develop the film, you can stick pins in the picture for me,' he said.

The roads gradually widened, we repeated our double run into the housing estate and then descended back into town. I thanked him for what had been the best bus ride I had enjoyed in years. He said: 'The bus hasn't been too bad today. Next time I'm on it I'll try bringing my own camera.'

Later that day, and by chance rather than design, I came across the other buses in the fleet.

They were P-registered Leyland Nationals.

Twenty-year Gap

Michael Fowler looks at the buses of two Lincolnshire operators two decades apart, turning the clock back to 1977 and comparing that period with the 1990s.

Above:
Lest there be any doubt, the National Holidays advert confirms that this is indeed a 1977 view of a Lincolnshire RoadCar Lodekka. It's a 1959 LD5G — a reminder that old buses are not purely a post-deregulation phenomenon — and this was its last year in service.

Left:
With the same multistorey car park in the background, a 1981 Atlantean has one common feature with the earlier Lodekka — bodywork by ECW. New to Trent, it joined the RoadCar fleet in 1995. Note how the company had changed its trading name, from Lincolnshire to RoadCar.

Above right:
There were second-hand buses in the Lincolnshire fleet 20 years ago, in the shape of 10 ex-Scottish Bus Group Bristol VRTs. This one was new to Central SMT in 1969 and moved south to Lincolnshire four years later.

Right:
Second-hand buses play a bigger part in the present-day RoadCar fleet. This one-time Merseyside PTE Atlantean was bought from Nottingham Omnibus in 1995. It was new in 1978 and has MCW bodywork.

Below:
New recruits to the ranks of Lincolnshire's drivers in 1977 would have found themselves confronted with this 1960 Bristol MW, unusual in being a six-cylinder MW6G rather than the company's standard MW5G. It served as a driver training vehicle from 1973 to 1979 and carried a non-standard version of NBC's corporate livery with white window surrounds. There's a strange irony in a non-PSV being painted in a brighter livery than was used for revenue-earning buses.

Above;
The need for training goes on, and in the mid-1990s a 1978 Bristol LH6L is filling the role of driver training unit.

Below:
Old-established independent Hornsby of Ashby bought this Leyland Atlantean from Maidstone & District in 1975. It had bodywork by Metro-Cammell. The company has been running double-deckers since the late 1940s.

Above right:
Two Roe-bodied Atlanteans were purchased by Hornsby from Yorkshire Rider in 1994. They dated from 1977 and were generally similar to a Roe-bodied Atlantean which Hornsby had bought new in 1978.

Right:
An unusual coach owned by Hornsby in 1977 was this Bedford J2 with Caetano body. It was new in 1976.

Below:
A couple of ex-London buses joined the 1990s Hornsby fleet, including this 1977 Leyland National, rebuilt to single-door layout.

Left:
The author's first encounter with open-top buses was at Weston-super-Mare where Bristol Omnibus introduced a quartet of FS Lodekkas in 1961. This view illustrates the cream livery which provided a striking contrast to the standard Tilling green of the remainder of the fleet.
ALL PHOTOGRAPHS BY THE AUTHOR

Some Open-toppers I Have Known

Martin S. Curtis takes a look back at his involvement with open-top buses, both as an observer and an operator.

As somebody who has always been fascinated by transport and who later decided to extend this interest into a profession, I realised long ago that it was necessary to establish a fine but distinct line between what is work and what is not. Failure to recognise this distinction can deflect one's attention from professional responsibilities and impair sound commercial judgement.

Having said that, and while acknowledging that to reflect on the past and enjoy older vehicles may not be compatible with planning and operating a modern public transport network, there are nevertheless occasions when sheer enthusiasm and serious business requirements can comfortably overlap. And an area which for me has proved both very commercially successful while offering unceasing interest has been the provision of open-top bus services.

My first encounter with open-top buses was at Weston-super-Mare. Having been born and raised in Bristol, the activities of both Bristol Omnibus and Bristol Commercial Vehicles couldn't fail to attract my attention. In those days most of my journeys of any length were made by bus as my family, like the majority in the 1950s and early 1960s, still lacked a car, and a visit to the seaside some 20 miles away remained a great adventure.

In 1961 Bristol Omnibus received four convertible ECW-bodied FS6G Lodekkas for use at Weston. These

vehicles immediately captured my imagination as they purred along the sea front from the Old Pier (involving a tricky reversing manoeuvre) to Uphill, a most delightful village on the edge of the town. And not only were these buses open-toppers — what was equally striking was their all-over cream livery. At first Bristol fleetnames in gold block capital letters were carried but the Weston coat of arms was soon substituted, despite these buses being company-owned with no direct council connections. So before me would appear the Bristol-ECW shape with which I was so familiar, but wearing a delightfully rich cream instead of the normal green with cream stripes — and with no top!

A ride upstairs was exhilarating and also offered engine and gearbox sounds from both within and outside the vehicle simultaneously, often echoing off buildings as they were passed.

The sea breeze blew everywhere, so small traces of sand were always present throughout, including in the lower saloon interiors which were finished in standard green trim. As a young boy, if it was necessary to travel inside because the top deck was full (which was always a disappointment) I felt compelled to stare at the cream bonnet or platform lest I forgot that I was not riding on a standard Lodekka. Good loads were common in those days, even late at night when these buses continued to run long after sunset.

The impression these buses made was profound and

some years later, when I found myself first conducting (which itself requires considerably more care on an open-top bus!) and later driving these vehicles, I developed a new respect for them as I found them to be the best Lodekkas — and indeed among the best buses — I have ever had the pleasure to drive.

As the popularity of the Weston open-toppers grew, with open-top tours added to the operation, 1973 saw the arrival of two more Lodekkas. These were second-hand LD6Bs from Crosville and these too received similar cream livery, but I never considered them to be quite as good as the original FS types.

Of course, after discovering the Weston open-top FSs I became aware that other open-top buses existed and among those operating in the southwest was a batch of nine Metro-Cammell-bodied convertible Atlanteans working with Devon General in the Torquay area. These too were built in 1961 and wore ivory livery relieved by Devon General dark red, almost the reverse of the company's normal livery. They were known as 'Sea Dogs' as each carried the name of a famous seafarer, an idea I was to remember and return to later.

When new, the Devon General convertibles were finished with ivory wheels to match the main body colour, though the wheels were soon changed to the company's standard dark red, no doubt to avoid the need for a repaint following routine wheel-changing. The lighter wheels always looked special and whilst any road vehicle operator knows dark-coloured wheels are easier to maintain, a well-cared-for group of specialised vehicles such as open-top buses can benefit from a little extra attention which contributes towards an exceptional appearance.

When the National Bus Company introduced light grey as its standard wheel colour for all vehicles as part of its corporate livery in 1972 it was doomed to failure because on the first wheel change after repaint — or simply in the course of normal wear —

wheels soon looked shabby and unkempt unless they received costly and time-consuming special attention. Only Eastern National managed — by a process of extra cleaning and painting — to maintain NBC's intended appearance on a large scale.

Back in Weston-super-Mare an upsurge of interest in open-top buses by the mid-1970s resulted in a seventh Bristol Lodekka arriving for open-top work. This vehicle differed considerably from the others since it was a former Bristol city services forward-entrance FLF model, converted to permanent open-top configuration. Furthermore, this bus, together with the earlier Weston Lodekka open-toppers, was outshopped in one of a range of curious liveries incorporating a bright colour on a white background. Each was intended to represent a former tram-operating town or city in the Bristol Omnibus Company's area and carried a motif and name in the Western series appropriate to each location. Accordingly the FLF wore dark blue and white, was named *Western Challenger*, and displayed a Concorde insignia to represent the City of Bristol.

These colours were lively and varied, albeit less than accurate in the tram livery sense. But most important of all, they failed in one fundamental respect in Weston: they were hard to spot. Weston sea front has a long expanse of uninterrupted promenade bordered largely by lawns. It was therefore possible to spot an oncoming open-top bus approaching from some considerable distance — up to three-quarters of a mile in some situations. Unfortunately, the new liveries acted as camouflage against the colourful sea front attractions, and the buses could no longer be recognised so easily until they were much nearer intending or potential passengers.

Since so much open-top traffic was (and still is) discretionary — with the decision to travel being made only moments before boarding — this difference was significant. The situation was highlighted even more by

Above:
The only FLF Lodekka open-topper operated by Bristol, photographed from Weston bus station in June 1979 with a school party aboard. Painted dark blue and white, it was supposed to represent a Bristol tram.

Below:
Roe-bodied Atlanteans which originated with King Alfred enabled the sea front services at Weston-super-Mare to be converted to one-man operation. Freshly painted cream, this bus heads for Uphill in July 1980.

an eighth open-top bus, still in rich cream livery, which had appeared in Weston to join the town's Lodekkas.

The vehicle in question was another Bristol, but not a Lodekka. It was GHT127, the famous 1941 K5G/ECW which had begun life as a tram replacement bus in Bristol during World War 2. It had passed to Brighton Hove & District in 1955 and, like a number of similar vehicles, had been rebuilt as an open-topper. In 1965 it moved again, to Thomas Bros at Port Talbot, but in 1969 was returned to Bristol Omnibus, where I first encountered it. After five years in store it was prepared for service once again and dispatched to Weston.

This K5G deserves an article to itself as it has become something of a legend, but suffice it to say here that it

Above:
Modernisation of the Weston open-top fleet came in 1984 with the arrival of more Leyland/Roe buses, this time brand-new convertible Olympians. *Sea Witch*, in blue and white, takes on passengers at the Old Pier.

Below:
The summer of 1983 was the first following the creation of Southern National Ltd, and the company's two convertible Bristol VRTs appear together at the King's Statue, Weymouth, having just been painted cream and green.

bus it will never operate successfully: only if operating (and maintenance) staff are committed to an unusual or non-standard vehicle will it continue to run smoothly in service.

One-man-operation (political correctness now demands we use the term one-person-operation) was beckoning, however, even on the sea front services in Weston-super-Mare, and thoughts moved to a new open-top fleet which could be operated safely without conductors. The Lodekkas were gradually withdrawn and dispersed among new owners — and surprisingly have survived, with several remaining in service around the country, including the FLF which in 1994 reappeared on a Bristol city tour. In the meantime GHT127 returned to a further period in store.

A new open-top bus fleet gradually took over at Weston from the end of 1979, but instead of replacement Bristol/ECW vehicles in the form of new convertible VRTs as seen elsewhere within the National Bus Company, a motley collection of second-hand Atlanteans and Fleetlines was acquired by Bristol Omnibus, cut down to open-top, and sent to Weston to maintain the sea front services. The company had apparently missed the chance to buy convertible VRTs when one large order had been placed by NBC for delivery during 1977/8, so former King Alfred buses were acquired ex-Hants & Dorset, along with vehicles from Maidstone & District and Midland Red. Indeed, the Devon General 'Sea Dog' Atlanteans had been requested at one stage, but these were not available.

These buses were far from new when they arrived at Weston and reliability was poorer than the Lodekkas (or even the K5G) which they replaced. But at least the livery lesson had been learned and cream was restored. It

was a vehicle I was to encounter on a number of occasions from then on. While at Weston in the 1970s it was not always popular with staff and was felt by many Weston drivers to be an obsolete curiosity which they did not appreciate having imposed on them. Several drivers found every excuse not to drive it if possible, but there were a few who persevered and considered it something of an achievement to keep it on the road. Here I learned an important lesson. If drivers dislike a

was in fact a slightly less rich shade of ivory than proper Tilling cream, but it was near enough.

The Daimler Fleetlines from Midland Red were short-lived but some of the Atlanteans were to remain in use for a surprisingly long time. Unfortunately, as part of the marketing effort during 1982, the Weston open-top services were repackaged and white and blue was adopted as the open-top livery. Of course these colours are often used more generally to represent coldness, and if open-top buses look cold, they become less inviting to intending passengers. Experience had by this time taught me that a bright cream (or indeed a sunny yellow) livery adds to the appeal of open-top buses, irrespective of the prevailing climatic conditions.

However, for me it was time to leave Weston-super-Mare and move to the Dorset coast where I became superintendent at Weymouth with Western National.

Here just one open-top bus was offered to visitors. This was deposited in Weymouth for the peak summer season during early June each year, following the annual pilgrimage to the Epsom Derby where so many open-top buses traditionally appear as grandstands. Once again I narrowly missed operating a Devon General Atlantean which had undertaken this role in previous years at Weymouth because in 1982 one of Western National/Devon General's new generation of open-top Bristol VRTs was allocated to Weymouth for the first time.

By this time NBC's standard liveries had been established for several years, but the Devon open-toppers were all finished in a well-proportioned NBC poppy red and white scheme, with much more white than standard. The naming tradition was perpetuated, and while Weymouth's visiting 'Sea Dog' Atlantean had

previously been renamed to assume a Dorset-based personality, the VRTs were dubbed Warship-class, as each carried the name of a battleship.

At the beginning of 1983 the Western National Omnibus Co was divided into four and the Weymouth and Bridport areas, for which I later became manager, passed to a new Southern National company. Movements of open-top buses between West Country resorts effectively ceased from this time, so when the music stopped and the new companies came into being, those vehicles allocated to depots at that time generally

Above:
Immediately following a repaint into the new livery, and with roof still in position, a Southern National convertible poses at Sutton Poyntz in 1983.

Below:
The similarity between the Bath and the Weymouth open-top livery can be judged by comparing VRTs from both fleets, posed side by side at the 1985 Bristol bus rally. Both were converted to open-top layout by Hants & Dorset Engineering earlier that year.

Left:
After a brief period in yellow, red and blue, the Bath Tour fleet operated by Badgerline adopted primrose, lime green and Brunswick green from 1989. With a full top-deck load *Dr William Oliver* guides visitors through the Georgian streets on a hot summer's afternoon.

Below left:
One of the more surprising open-top buses to appear in Bath was CentreWest's RMC1510 in full London red livery. Borrowed by Badgerline during May 1993 it is here viewed in The Circus.

continuing, but with the use of more appropriate local names, such as those of personalities connected with the area. Locally it was considered the most obvious choice would be that of King George III, whose statue towers over the centre of Weymouth and who was largely responsible for popularising the town as a resort.

Permission was sought from Buckingham Palace and while this was awaited with anticipation, we were certain that it would be just a formality — after all, public houses and railway engines had received similar names. We were therefore somewhat shocked when the Home Office intervened and forbade any use of the name King George III or of any other former monarch on our vehicles — and to this day I can only speculate on the reasons for this refusal. To my further regret, I carelessly related this story to a journalist friend who was working on a trade paper, only to be surprised shortly afterwards to discover the whole affair published in the press! I suppose I should have known better, but I was not amused by this embarrassment. Fortunately for me, my boss was.

These problems were soon forgotten, however, and after the local evening newspaper had organised a competition the names *Thomas Hardy* and *Lawrence of Arabia* were selected. The buses began a fairly intensive operation from Weymouth sea front to Bowleaze Cove and Sutton Poyntz or Osmington and Portland — and became extremely successful.

Although working in Weymouth, I was keeping in touch with developments in my old stamping grounds. Bristol Omnibus had extended open-top bus operation to the Georgian city of Bath, and although this World Heritage city continues to be one of Europe's most popular tourist destinations, during the early 1980s open-top bus operation away from a coastline remained very unusual outside of London.

became the ones owned by the appropriate company. When asked therefore if I wanted an open-topper from Devon, not only did I agree, but I suggested that two might be even more useful. And so it was that two S-registered VRT convertibles were allocated to Weymouth.

NBC standard liveries still prevailed, but in order to give a little more prominence to the new company (and as they were special vehicles) it was decided to repaint the open-toppers into a non-standard scheme of NBC green but with large areas of rich Tilling cream. The strict policy and enforcement of NBC's rigid livery code made this move rather daring at the time, but the attractive result, and the ability to apply all the marketing reasons for having cream open-top buses for the Weymouth Esplanade operation, meant that we got away with it!

Unfortunately, there was still trouble to come, since the tradition of naming these buses was felt worth

At Weston, the remaining Atlanteans were joined by a new fleet of six Roe-bodied convertible open-top Olympians in 1984, while the Bath open-top fleet included an ex-Hants & Dorset Atlantean and two former H&D/Southern Vectis convertible VRTs which had moved to Bath after a season at Weston. Still more open-toppers were needed, however, so further VRTs were rebuilt for both Weston and Bath by Hants & Dorset Engineering, which simultaneously was converting another VRT for use by Southern National at Weymouth, an L-registered bus and the first of its Series 2 VRTs to be so modified.

Weston's open-top bus livery remained blue and white and the vehicles were now named in a series with seashore associations, while Bath's open-toppers appeared in cream and green. The similarity in appearance of the latter to those vehicles running at Weymouth was a surprising coincidence, for not only was the style almost identical, but the shades too were very alike. Indeed the paint for the later conversions by Hants & Dorset Engineering for both the Weymouth and the Bath fleets literally came out of the same pot!

In 1985 Bristol Omnibus, itself divided into smaller units, began the introduction of Badgerline livery using strong green and yellow shades for its former Bristol Country division. Soon Badgerline evolved to become a separate company, which rapidly developed further to be among the most successful following NBC privatisation. At Bath the cream open-top bus livery which provided a strong contrast to the standard NBC leaf green was suddenly somewhat overwhelmed by the bright new Badgerline livery — but this was soon to change.

Much to my surprise I found myself leaving Weymouth to join the new Badgerline company in Bath, first in charge of operations and later as a director. The open-top livery of cream and green therefore seemed very familiar, but a prominent Bath coach operator, Roman City, was at that time being acquired and it was felt appropriate to extend the Roman City livery to the open-toppers in Bath, then numbering five VRTs and an Atlantean.

Roman City livery was much stronger than the previous cream, being composed of deep yellow with a rich red and dark blue skirt, following the layout used in Weymouth, but upswept at the rear.

I was never really happy with this scheme, and it provoked criticism from some of Bath's highly sensitive environmentalists as it didn't complement the city's architecture. It was also frequently confused with the red, yellow and blue of nearby City Line, as worn by Bristol Omnibus vehicles in Bristol.

The opportunity to correct this situation arose in 1989. From this time Badgerline had embarked on a close working relationship with tour specialist Guide Friday of Stratford-upon-Avon, who themselves ran open-top buses in many of Britain's heritage cities. In Bath, however, Guide Friday was to work in partnership with Badgerline and a brand-new, but very carefully considered, livery was introduced.

The style and layout were exactly as used on the Weymouth VRTs, with deep skirt colours to hide road dirt, but the shades of colour were adjusted. Dark Brunswick green was applied to the lower sections, akin to Guide Friday's house colour, while the main colour switched from cream to a deep and complicated primrose. A lime green waistband (and roof on the convertible) completed the arrangement, with Guide Friday corporate lettering styles used to portray the tour route. This livery was in effect a very rich cream and green, which restored a striking contrast to the standard Badgerline green and yellow. It also seemed more in keeping with the Bath stone of the city's Georgian buildings, and while the frequency and number of tour buses in Bath have caused complaint from local residents from time to time, the Bath Tour livery developed a strong following.

Such was the attention lavished on the Bath Tour fleet we even decided that we could afford to break the rules on wheel colour (which had been plain grey until 1990) and introduced primrose wheels with lime green hubs (Scottish Bus Group style) which, so long as they were not allowed to deteriorate, provided the finishing touch to the immaculate appearance of the open-top fleet.

The success of the Bath Tour operation was so great that passenger loadings soared, with up to 150,000 being carried by the Badgerline/Guide Friday operation each year. Inevitably such success attracted competition and two rival concerns were soon running topless buses in Bath. This prompted more complaints from residents who objected (and still do) to so many tourists being carried around the city, although their contribution to the local economy is also recognised by many more.

Badgerline's open-top fleet in Bath had grown to no fewer than 10 Bristol VRTs with ECW bodywork by the end of 1991, including examples acquired from sister Badgerline group companies City Line, South Wales Transport and Western National. These worked alongside the VRTs converted by H&D Engineering earlier, and the pair obtained from Southern Vectis. One of the Vectis buses was destroyed by fire during December 1992 and was quickly replaced by a further convertible from Western National. The former Western National vehicles were of course part of the S-registered batch supplied to Western National/Devon General, like those used by Southern National at Weymouth.

Not deterred by the trouble in Weymouth, and again with assistance from the local newspaper, competitions were organised to name each of Badgerline's Bath open-top fleet after historical characters from Bath's past. Naturally, permission to use each name was carefully sought (and there were no refusals this time) so names such as *Minerva*, *Beau Nash*, *Jane Austen* and *I. K. Brunel* proudly adorned the vehicles.

Although, as mentioned above, the Bath open-top operation in which I was involved grew to include 10 VRTs, there was one further Bristol/ECW bus, built to permanent open-top configuration, which has regularly appeared on Bath Tour work. This was none other than

GHT127, by then well over 50 years old and much sought after by drivers and guides who delighted in the celebrity status held by this remarkable vehicle. Having been in store for a number of years, it was acquired from City Line and in 1990 refurbished and painted in full Bath Tour livery. It quickly constituted a major attraction for both visitors and transport enthusiasts alike.

Open-top bus operation is rather different from other kinds of local bus service, and requires a degree of specialisation in order to succeed — whether on a seaside route or a city tour. This is not least because so much passenger traffic is generated by the vehicles' appearance and ease of access to a boarding point, since a very high proportion of passengers decide to ride spontaneously when an open-topper comes into view. Once aboard, however, open-top-deck travel can offer unrivalled views, and is for many a unique experience.

Above:
Never failing to attract attention — and good loads — is Badgerline's 1941 Bristol K5G/ECW. This remarkable vehicle has been encountered by the author at various times during his career, most recently working on summer Saturdays on the Bath Tour, with Guide Friday couriers providing a commentary.

And with top decks full to capacity — and not just in the summer months — people like me could occasionally step back from the hive of activity involved in bus operation to admire these heavily-laden vehicles and the success they have brought. I have been fortunate, having been able to do this in respect of a number of open-toppers I have known.

When Duple was Dominant

Geoff Mills illustrates a cross-section of the postwar products of Duple, which for a lengthy period was Britain's leading coach manufacturer.

Above left:
At the start of the 1950s half-cab coaches were distinctly old-fashioned. Typical of the last generation of Duple's half-cab bodies was this 37-seater supplied to Western National in 1951. It was one of 38 on 30ft-long Bristol LL6B chassis which were Western National's last half-cab coaches. It is seen in London in 1962.
ALL PHOTOGRAPHS BY THE AUTHOR

Left:
Most early underfloor-engined coaches had bodies which retained styling cues from earlier half-cab vehicles, such as the gently curved waist on this 1953 Royal Tiger for Suttons of Clacton-on-Sea. This body style was called the Ambassador.

Below:
The combination of Bedford SB chassis and Duple Vega body was popular with small fleets in the 1950s. Cream Bus Service of Stamford was one of many small firms to run Vegas. Duple bodies of this period were built at Hendon.

Above right:
The Donnington body was built by Duple (Midland) at Loughborough and looked rather austere with its straight waist and shallow windows. This is an early example, one of 10 supplied in 1958 to BET subsidiary Timpsons of Catford, London. Later Donningtons had curved windscreens and deeper side windows.

Right:
Black & White Motorways of Cheltenham pursued an individualistic policy, with non-standard body mouldings and features such as the sun visor and winged motif above it. This is a late Britannia body, dating from 1961.

Below:
For front-engined chassis Duple built this style of body in the late 1950s and early 1960s. It was called the Super Vega on Bedford SB or the Yeoman on the Ford Thames 570E. Suttons of Clacton-on-Sea bought two Yeomans in 1962.

Above:
The takeover of Burlingham by Duple in 1961 saw some attractive but short-lived designs being produced at Burlingham's Blackpool factory, now known as Duple (Northern). This was a Dragonfly, a model of which only six were built. It was developed from the more common Firefly. The Dragonfly was built on 36ft underfloor-engined chassis; the Firefly on front-engined Bedfords, Fords and Albion Victors. Samuelson of London operated four AEC Reliances with Dragonfly bodies.

Above left:
The Continental, also built at Blackpool on 36ft-long mid-engined chassis, was rather more successful than the short-lived Dragonfly. Osborne's of Tollesbury took delivery of this smart example in 1963. By the end of the 1960s all of Duple's bodybuilding activities would be carried out at Blackpool.

Left:
The new Bella range of bodies, introduced from 1962, set the standard for Duple styling for much of the 1960s. The reverse-rake pillar towards the rear was a hallmark of the range. The original Bella Vista (Bedford VAS), Bella Vega (Bedford SB) and Trooper (Ford Thames) were joined by additional models over the following years, including the Bella Venturer, seen here on a 1965 Bedford VAM5 owned by Mulleys of Ixworth.

Above:
As the Bella style evolved the reverse-rake pillar was abandoned, as demonstrated by this Commander on a 36ft AEC Reliance operated by Cook of Biggleswade. New in 1968, it was a 51-seater.

Right:
The Commander range underwent a number of facelifts, resulting in this crisp-looking coach with fashionable peaked dome which was operated by Maidstone & District. M&D had traditionally been a Reliance buyer, but this was one of a dozen Leyland Leopards delivered in 1968.

Below right:
The Viceroy was the design which took Duple into the 1970s. It was fitted to a wide range of chassis, including the Bedford VAL. Southern Vectis operated VALs on Isle of Wight tours.

In 1972 Duple launched the Dominant, which would appear in a variety of styles over the following decade. One of the most impressive was the high-floor Goldliner, developed to offer increased luggage storage under the floor. The most unusual Goldliners were 10 built on rear-engined Dennis Falcons for the National Bus Company. These were used on National Express services by a number of NBC subsidiaries, including West Yorkshire Road Car.

Left:
The Dominant was succeeded in 1982 by the Laser and the highfloor Caribbean. In 1983 National Travel East added five Caribbeans to its fleet. These were unusual for an NBC operator in being on Volvo rather than Leyland chassis.

Below left:
Both the Caribbean and the Laser were short-lived, and in 1985 they were replaced by what was to be Duple's final coach body range, the 320 and 340 — the numbers signifying their overall height in centimetres. Lothian, a long-standing Duple user, bought two 55-seat 340s in 1986. They were on Leyland Tiger chassis.

Above:
The Duple 425 Integral was launched at the 1984 Motor Show and featured a rear-mounted Cummins L10 engine. Skill's of Nottingham bought two in 1991. The figure 425 indicated the body's drag coefficient — 0.425 — and not its overall height.

Below:
When Duple closed in 1991 Plaxton bought the rights to its range of bodies, and in 1992 built a batch of 25 320s on Leyland Tiger chassis. These carried Plaxton badges — visible above the grille — and this model was known as the Plaxton 321. The figures are carried vertically on the badge below the Plaxton name. The first 321 was a demonstrator for Yeates, the Loughborough-based coach dealer.

Coaches of Teme Valley Motors of Leintwardine, Herefordshire, lined up awaiting school time. For three years Jowitt regularly drove the second on the left or the second on the right and they seldom did anything except schools.
ALL PHOTOGRAPHS BY THE AUTHOR

SCHOOLS

Robert E. Jowitt, in the dual role of bus driver and bus photographer, studies school transport from inside and out — from the difficulties of being a disciplinarian at the wheel to the delights of uniforms in days of yore.

'Amy, will you sit down properly, please. How many times have I told you?' 'Daniel, bring that conker here and give it to me and sit down in the front where I can keep an eye on you.' 'Tracey, don't drop your lemonade bottle on the floor.' How many times, between 8 and 9am and 3.30 and 4.30pm, have I cried such exhortations to 40 or 50 brats, sorry, I mean schoolchildren, and how many other drivers in how many other ageing and battered buses and coaches have shouted the same as twice daily in term time all over the British Isles a vast fleet of buses engages in the contract transport of schoolchildren, workings known in the bus operating world simply and succinctly as 'schools'.

If for hundreds of years pupils were prepared to foot slog their way to their places of education as summed up graphically by Shakespeare as 'creeping like snails unwillingly to school,' the dawn of mechanised transport brought about a revolution in school travel habits. I am not sure if the bicycle can be included in mechanised transport but 'what happened behind the school bike sheds' has certainly entered into British folklore and possibly has not been without consequence on British history and statistics, though in this present entirely motorised age fraught with perils for cycle riders, the bike sheds have now been relegated to museum-piece status.

Anyway, setting aside the dubious claims of the

bicycle, there can be little doubt that after the introduction of tramways and then buses, even if many pupils continued to follow the Bard's precept of creeping unwillingly, many others took to tram or bus especially in urban areas. Lionel Wiener's erudite work *Passenger Tickets*, implies that scholars' needs were recognised at a fairly early date. In rural areas the case was more difficult and Shanks's pony was generally the rule, though in the depths of Hardy's heaths in Dorset a hen-house-like erection was set on a quarry truck chassis to convey outlying pupils behind a narrow-gauge steam loco to the nearest village school. This China Clay initiative merited a column in *Railway Magazine*, but in due time was replaced by the precursors — Bedford OBs and suchlike — of the school transport scene which we still enjoy or suffer today.

I never went to school on a school bus; my parents always had a car, even in the later 1940s, which took me to various infant bear gardens, and then in 1950 I started at prep school where most of the pupils were boarders so there was no question of buses. One or two of the minority day boys, however, did travel in and out on ordinary service buses. This being Winchester, these, of course, were King Alfred buses. Occasionally I was asked to tea with one of these day boys and would thus travel on a King Alfred bus and, being overexcited by the novelty, tended to be cheeky to the conductor... and be duly reprimanded.

If my prep school was thus no more than peripherally involved with King Alfred buses, we had some dealings with a KA veteran. My school now and then played matches against West Hill Park, another Hampshire prep school which we chose to deride because its team came in a very small Dennis bus which in our eyes was ludicrously antediluvian. It later transpired that one of the Chisnell sons (operators of King Alfred) had been at West Hill Park and that West Hill Park had acquired one of the 1931 18-seater Dennis buses for team transport. The subsequent career of this bus, via Vernons Pools and a Yorkshire vet on TV, to its eventual return to the fold of the Friends of King Alfred Buses is well known and needs no further comment here.

It is, however, worth giving further details about King Alfred's involvement in schools. There are no doubt earlier records of such transport than those referring to King Alfred, but I was for many years resident in Winchester and therefore studied the history of the King Alfred buses and heard tales of school operations from the men who had worked them in the 1920s.

There were, of course, Sunday School outings in Leyland charabancs. But these were sporadic, indeed probably no more than once a year. King Alfred, however, was at an early stage involved in regular school runs. The well-known academy for young ladies known as St Swithun's was first of all established in the city itself in a building of splendid red and white Butterfield style brick (now housing the County Library) but, as it expanded, various large villas on the heights of St Giles' Hill, east of the city, were acquired to house the increasing number of boarders.

King Alfred was called upon to provide transport between the school and the boarding houses. The Delaunay Belleville shooting brakes which operated the service, echoing with enthusiastic but genteel descriptions of hockey and prep in the style of Angela Brazil, were well used to this route, for they had worked it from the very start of the firm's operations, carrying officers and men between the World War 1 camps beyond St Giles' Hill and the delights of the city and echoing to broader tales — and perhaps bloodier — than those related in the dulcet tones of St Swithun's girls. In their peacetime role the Delaunays were known by the drivers as 'satchel cars'.

In 1932 the school abandoned the cramped premises in North Walls for brand-new buildings on Morn Hill, not far from the site of the World War 1 camps. This was not the end of the satchel cars, but henceforth their role was reversed; they took the day girls up from the city in the morning and down again in the afternoon. Though I seem to have failed to ascertain whether this service was curtailed during World War 2 (I suspect it was), it carried on afterwards until the end of King Alfred Motor Services in 1973, whereafter I failed to observe how or if at all it was replaced.

Meanwhile with the Atlee Government which followed the war, the Welfare State blossomed into national health and so on, and the education part of this programme produced various schools for Winchester in the usual biscuit-tin and shoe-box architecture, with transport provided by, among others, King Alfred. This resulted in vast double-decker Leyland PD1s and PD2s and then Atlanteans, plunging out into the depths of sparsely populated countryside on routes which barely merited a single-decker. These buses had the interesting habit, when working outwards empty to the schools in the afternoon to collect the 'little angels', of driving up Winchester High Street, a practice which had been forbidden to normal service buses since the introduction of the Road Traffic Act in 1930.

As may be apparent, some of these services started off as 'schools' and then as they travelled further they became ordinary stage carriage routes as well, though woe betide the luckless passenger who boarded them... There is only a very thin line dividing buses which work school contracts from regular stage carriage services which operate 'during school terms only'.

Tucked away in the more remote parts of the country — and perhaps even in towns too — are buses which emerge only twice a day, just for schools, and therefore don't appear in the 'hols' at all. At least one Welsh

Facing page:
Primrose Motors of Leominster, Herefordshire, keep this bus outstationed on the top of Clee Hill simply to do morning and evening school runs. The rest of the time it sits among the sheep.

Facing page, inset:
School runs often provide an extension of life for second-hand city buses. This fine specimen from Johnson's of Henley-in-Arden speeds into Warwick on a school run in January 1993.

Left:
Transport for the Bournemouth School for Girls called for an intensive operation by Corporation vehicles. A 1959 Sunbeam MF2B trolleybus with Weymann body loads in March 1966, with its passengers sporting a fine array of classic school hats.

Top:
Another array of classic school hats in Manchester in October 1965. It would be nice to imagine they have just descended from the trolleybus in the background.

Above;
Splendid examples of school blazers, with a 1946 Bradford Corporation Karrier W, seen here with new East Lancs body 20 years later.

operator, owning only one coach, worked on this basis for many years.

This may seem fairly idyllic, but 'schools' are not without problems. Let us return to King Alfred. In 1966 the children from Highcliffe, a between-the-wars estate, one day vandalised their bus so badly that Mr Bob Chisnell (son of the firm's founder) withdrew the service on the spot. The Highcliffe kids, while enjoying a day of unwonted liberty, retaliated by hurling clods of earth at the regular Highcliffe service bus as it passed through the estate.

Worse was to follow. Several 'schools' in the Winchester area were operated by Horace Taylor of Sutton Scotney, a village a few miles north of Winchester. Horace Taylor himself was a basso profundo who enjoyed many decades of success in the Winchester Amateur Operatic Society, whose performances were also graced at intervals by members of the Chisnell family. Taylors of Sutton Scotney had long played a part in the Winchester bus scene, but suffice it here to say that while King Alfred faded away Taylors' business increased; and if this was mainly in luxury coaching it was also in 'schools', the vehicles involved in these being double-deckers which appeared to be of Scottish origin.

It was on one of these on the top deck that some wretched child let off a firework. The driver stopped there and then and refused to drive any further.

There was an enormous outcry in the local press. Should he have stopped or shouldn't he? But what else could he do? I would have stopped just like him. I agreed with him entirely at the time from, as it were, a civilian point of view and recently I have agreed with him all the more. As I related in a previous *Buses Yearbook*, I have over the last few years been engaged — as will be apparent from my words in this *Buses Yearbook* — in driving buses myself, the financial rewards of authorship and bus photography proving inadequate to feed a growing family, and most of this work has been on schools… Our local firm had to step into the breach caused by the inability of another operator and I thus occasionally had to drive a service known by the dramatic title of 'girls' town'. Exciting as this may sound, what it really meant was that, though the large Roman Catholic school was mixed, its bus transport was sexually segregated and this bus conveyed girls from the school to the bus station in the county town (let it be nameless!). I was warned by another driver: 'If the girls ask if they can smoke at the back of the bus let them, otherwise they'll slash the seats'. Our boss had already withdrawn another service from that same county town for the same reason. What could I do except let the Catholic maidens smoke?

A schools driver is in a very difficult position, driving in sometimes dreadful weather conditions and having to play the role of disciplinarian as well. I have sometimes had to stop my bus four or five times in a 45min run to repeat a few simple requests such as 'Will you please stay in the same seat and sit down,' 'Don't throw empty bottles about' and 'Stop fighting' or just 'Shut up.' Usually time and time again to the same children who seem incapable of understanding or memorising the easiest order. Perhaps it is their parents' fault? Such children are well known and blacklisted by all bus drivers, so it isn't just me. There are a lot of parents too, whose children don't go on buses, who are blacklisted by bus drivers for incredibly inconsiderate parking. In this area the mothers with the maroon Morris and the Renault Space Wagon are famous and have more than once paralysed the entire bus evacuation of a local High School.

Other motorists are just as bad. I remember particularly an offensive man in a fat blue Ford whom I encountered when I was going uphill on a single track road. He pulled to his left a bit and sat there, and I sat there too because I could not squeeze through without taking out the side of my bus on a nearside rock. After we had both sat for some minutes he got out and I pointed out to him the fact that I could not pass him and he said I was being deliberately obstructive. I said I was not prepared to back the coach with 40 children down a twisting single track road for a quarter of a mile when there was a wide space only 50 yards behind him. Once or twice he got back into his car and thought about it and once or twice he got out again and gave me his views on bus drivers. Eventually he backed, erratically, the necessary 50 yards. I was a quarter of an hour late for the rest of the run — and this was just after one of those school bus disasters in the newspapers. There were a lot of anxious mothers awaiting my coming. How inconsiderate can you be?

Quite apart from the hazards presented by children and motorists, the profession (if that is the correct term) of part-time bus driver is a precarious one itself, subject to the whims of education authorities and their budgets and probably to still higher authority which may know very little of what really happens in the wild woods where the school buses run. Very lately our local contracts were up for tender mainly on account of seat belt laws resulting in my local company losing several routes and I found myself liable to be deprived of driving from the end of term. Fortunately for me the

Above:
The 1930 Road Traffic Act forbade buses in public service from using Winchester High Street, but 40 years later it was still in use as a short-cut for specials running empty to pick up at schools west of the city. Here are two King Alfred buses doing just this, with a 1959 AEC/Park Royal Bridgemaster in the lead (behind a choice VW) and a similar AEC in pursuit. The area has long since been pedestrianised.

contracts were won by another local firm for which I was already driving occasional stage carriage, so I was able to become an outstation and stick to my same route simply in different livery.

Regardless of such problems, I must say I believe that there are many worse occupations in life than driving 'schools', but I sometimes look back with nostalgia to the days when I simply photographed school buses and their passengers with no care or thought for whether they were contract or stage carriage, and cared far less about what the poor driver thought...

Unlike the successors to the satchel car girls, school children on the continent in the past three or four decades have not generally worn uniform, even if they

Right:
The relationship between King Alfred Motor Services and St Swithun's School for young ladies lasted half a century. In 1972, only months before the demise of King Alfred, a 1959 Bridgemaster deposits St Swithun's day girls in the latest trendy caps in Winchester Broadway.

Below:
School specials — at various angles — in City Road, Winchester, in 1972. The King Alfred Atlantean and Renown plus the Hants & Dorset Lodekka have picked up children from schools on the west of Winchester to drop some of them here to catch other buses — or to walk — and to take the rest on along the regular routes.

Above:
In Winchester in 1972 schoolchildren are being disgorged from a 1955 King Alfred Leyland Tiger Cub while two girls from Winchester County High School stride out in the latest trendy uniform — one bedecked with a straw boater as well.

Left:
A quarter of a century on from the Bradford picture, school blazers are still in force, but married to grey flannels and clumpy shoes. The bus is an ex-Southend Transport Leyland National working for Ludlows in Halesowen in 1993.

Below left:
Two Ludlows Nationals serving to transport scholars in the 1990s interpretation of school uniform where a Benetton shirt is quite OK — if you can get away with it.

wearing quasi-military uniform with peaked forage caps of the type favoured still in my youth and perhaps even today by German university students; but nearly all the other foreign schoolchildren I ever beheld, wore just what they pleased.

The situation in England is still in many cases rather different. While a French bus labelled 'transport des enfants' will disgorge a whole fashion parade, the widespread English insistence on uniform fortunately prevents competitive dressing, even if the days of the school cap and felt hat are long gone. Nowadays, of course, most sixth formers are in colleges and no longer included in secondary schools so they can dress as they choose, just as foreign students do, and not necessarily with very beautiful results, though this may depend on the eye of the beholder.

I drive sixth form college students now and then, and I have to remember

did in earlier years. In Werner Menninghaus's excellent book *Strassenbahnen in Lippe-Detmold und in Paderborner Land* is a magnificent photograph taken *circa* 1900 of a pack of schoolgirls boarding a tram all

this maxim, for I admit my taste in fashion is behind the times. On the other hand, while I deplore their tendency to forget their passes or to evade paying the fare, as the case may be, I can say in their favour that they usually behave in quite a docile manner and it makes a pleasant change from those neatly uniformed little dears to whom I have habitually to shout, 'Amy, will you sit down,' and 'Daniel, come and sit in the front where I can keep an eye on you.' Roll on the holidays!

Above left:
This covey of girls in Heidelberg in 1963 — they may be straight out of school and waiting to catch their trams home, though the absence of any school bags suggests that they are merely out on a spree — effectively depicts the lack of uniforms and the freedom of attire allowed to German schoolchildren as observed by Jowitt in the early 1960s. On the left is a Duwag articulated car of 1961, and beside it an Oberrheinsche Eisenbahn interurban built by Fuchs in 1928.

Left:
School's out for summer, even if the younger members of this group have yet to experience the joys of education. The Porto tram was built in 1909, and was still going strong in 1976 when this photograph was taken.

Left:
Dennis launched its new double-decker as the Lance in 1995, quickly renaming it the Arrow in 1996. Nottingham was the first operator to buy double-deck Lances, taking four with Northern Counties Palatine II bodies. They are used on park-and-ride services.
ALL PHOTOGRAPHS BY DAVID BARROW UNLESS SPECIFIED OTHERWISE

NOTTINGHAM
in the Nineties

Nottingham City Transport runs a varied fleet. **David Barrow** illustrates a selection of the municipally-owned company's buses.

Above right:
Nottingham introduced a new livery in 1994, based on the scheme used on its park-and-ride fleet. One of the first repaints was a 1986 Leyland Lion with Northern Counties body.

Right:
Most recent small buses have had Mercedes chassis. This is an 811D with Alexander body.

Top:
Six Scania L113 Axcess-ultralows are used on a route which passes the Queens Medical Centre on the outskirts of the city. They have bodies by Wright of Ballymena. This bus, with appropriate 113 registration, was the original Axcess-ultralow demonstrator.

Above:
There are 13 Volvo B6s in the fleet, all with Alexander Dash bodies. Nottingham's first Dennis Dart was delivered at the end of 1996.

Right:
In 1994 Nottingham bought its first Optare MetroRider. It now operates 24.

Above:
Volvo has been the main choice for both double- and single-deck buses since 1983. The latest are B10Bs with bodywork by Alexander and, as seen here in city centre traffic, Plaxton.

Left:
In the early 1990s Nottingham bought a number of Scania double-deckers, both new and second-hand. Alexander R-type bodywork is fitted to this N113 which is a former Scania demonstrator.

Below:
In 1994 a 20-year-old Atlantean was fitted with a new East Lancs Sprint body and allocated to the South Notts fleet. It seats 45. P. D. Scott

The Other Highland

Alistair Douglas takes a look at the last years of a long-vanished Lanarkshire independent which, with scant heed for geographical exactitude, traded as Highland Bus Service.

Coatbridge is one of Scotland's largest towns. An important iron and steel centre in the North Lanarkshire coalfield, its grim streets were for many years a damning indictment of the effects of the industrial revolution. Today most of the central area has been demolished and replaced by car parks and supermarkets to such an extent that the town has now become almost a caricature of the worst of modern urban developments.

All the coal mines have gone, together with much of the heavy industry (although it was one of the surviving Coatbridge firms which built the chassis frames for the Leyland National railcars), but the excellent Summerlee industrial museum will give the visitor a good insight into how things were.

My first visit to Coatbridge was in the early 1950s. I scarcely noticed the depressing surroundings, being far too interested in the fascinating transport scene. Glasgow Corporation's stately Coronation and Cunarder trams rumbled through the streets on services stretching out from Glasgow to Coatbridge's much more salubrious neighbour, Airdrie. Among them scurried some incredibly ancient-looking box-like single-deck buses. Some of the latter were in the smart blue livery of Baxter's Bus Service. Others were in red and cream and carried a curiously inappropriate name — Highland.

I was with a group of Ian Allan locospotters seeking out a local engine shed and saw less of these buses than I would have wished. By the time I was able to return for a longer visit the Baxter fleet had been modernised, but, fortunately, Highland was still running many of the distinctive buses I remembered glimpsing on my first trip. In those days we did not have the wealth of published information available now, and it was some time before I learned more of the origins of this interesting company.

John Carmichael had started operations from Glenmavis, a mining village near Coatbridge, but by 1931 was running local services in Dunbartonshire from a base in Helensburgh, as well as a service thence to Glasgow. He had plans, which may never have materialised, to run long-distance services into Argyll and, accordingly, adopted the trading name West Highland Motor Services. In 1932 the Dunbartonshire services and some vehicles were sold to Central SMT. The fleetname was shortened to Highland and the operation of services from Coatbridge to Kilsyth and Annathill and from Glasgow to Annathill continued under this name from a base in Airdrie. The Glasgow service and several more vehicles were sold to Alexanders in 1933. A move was made to Greenfoot Garage near Glenboig, from which the company continued to operate until 1966 when it was acquired, *in toto* this time, by Alexander (Midland). By then new services had been developed in the growing new town of Cumbernauld.

The earliest known bus in the fleet was a 14-seat GMC. Four Clydes were purchased between 1925 and 1930 and all of these later passed to another Lanarkshire operator, Hamilton Jackson of Auchenheath. The Clyde was built in Lanarkshire by a Wishaw company,

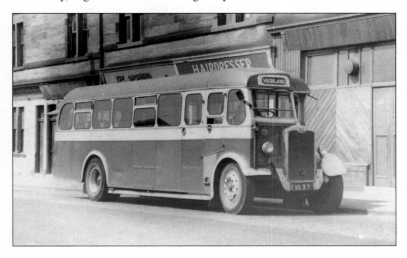

Left:
An Albion Valkyrie CX13 with Pickering body which had been new in 1946. By 1961, when this photograph was taken in Coatbridge, it had been rebuilt with rubber-mounted windows. It lasted until 1965.

MacKay & Jardine, which still exists as a car dealer within the Park of Hamilton group.

Also owned were several Gilfords, most of which went to Central SMT who quickly passed them on to Western SMT which already had vehicles of this make. However, Albions were Carmichael's first choice from the early days until they ceased to be obtainable. One Leyland Tiger TS8 was purchased new in 1938 (and resold in 1949) and second-hand Leylands were

Above:
An Albion Valiant CX39N with a second-hand body of unknown origin approaches Highland's Greenfoot garage in 1961 on its way to Coatbridge.

Below:
Another Pickering-bodied CX13 in the Highland fleet, but one which had been new in 1945 to Hanson of Huddersfield. It joined Highland in 1949. It is seen in Coatbridge in 1962 and survived to be acquired by Alexander (Midland) in 1966.

purchased in increasing numbers as suitable Albions became harder to find. However, the fleet acquired by Midland in 1966 still included 10 Albions. A solitary Dennis Lancet was owned for a time, and a former A1 Service AEC Regal ran briefly in 1958.

When I first knew the fleet, Albions predominated and they were not nearly as old as they looked. A magnificent 1932 PW65, WG1448, must have been around but I saw it only after it had been sold and preserved in the colours of its original owner, Alexanders. There were also two former Glasgow Corporation CX25s which had been new in 1939. The others dated from no earlier than 1945, despite their elderly looks.

Most had Pickering bodies. The angular utilitarian appearance of these bodies had not been improved by rebuilding. However, the mechanics at Greenfoot Garage obviously knew what they were about as they kept their ageing charges running despite their having been built at a time when materials were not always what they might have been and the problems they must have experienced in obtaining spares for Albion models long out of production.

There were already some second-hand Leyland PS1s in the fleet and more were acquired in 1960/61. Two short Leopards were bought new in 1961 and more were to follow. An 8ft-wide PS2/5 from the Ribble fleet in 1963, and a 1940 TS8 (with 1951 Alexander body)

Right:
Seen in the workshop which kept the company's old Albions soldiering on is a CX13 with Duple body, one of a pair bought new in 1948. This photograph was taken in 1964 and this coach was withdrawn in the following year.

Below:
A rather more modern Albion in the shape of a Victor FT39AL with Duple body. It is seen in Hamilton in 1964 on a private hire. It had been bought new by Highland in 1955.

Above:
Rare Strachan bodywork is fitted to this Victor. It started life in Glasgow with Lowland Motorways and operated for Highland between 1962 and 1966.

Below:
Several Leyland Tiger PS1s with Burlingham bodies were acquired from Western SMT in the period 1959-61. One is seen in Coatbridge in 1960.

acquired from Western SMT in 1964 added further variety. The growth of Cumbernauld new town was increasing the vehicle requirement and this was no doubt a factor in the decision to acquire no fewer than six Glasgow Corporation Worldmasters in 1965. These were to be the last additions to the fleet before Midland took control.

Some double-deckers were owned, although only single-deckers were used on the Coatbridge services. The first recorded was an ex-Southdown TD1 Titan. This had been followed by some ex-Glasgow Albions and then PD1 and PD2 Titans from Ribble and, in 1965, an ex-Western PD1. One new 'decker, a PD3, arrived in

1962 for use in Cumbernauld.

Albions were also favoured for the coach fleet and even when supplies of real Albions were drying up, the Leyland-ised Aberdonian was chosen. However, one Leyland Tiger Cub was purchased to become the flagship of the coach fleet in 1960.

The sale of the business to Midland did not see any immediate dramatic changes. The garage at Greenfoot remained in use and, apart from a change in the legal lettering, the vehicles were as before, not even carrying the fleetnumbers allotted by Midland.

Slowly, though, the newer vehicles began to appear in Midland blue and several Midland PS1s, PD1s and PD2s were drafted in to replace older buses. Eventually, in December 1967, the Greenfoot site was vacated and operations were transferred to a new depot built by Midland in Cumbernauld.

By this time most of the older vehicles had gone without ever losing their Highland identity. One Albion Valiant, FVA854, was sold for preservation — and has now been preserved for longer than it ran in revenue-earning service — while two ex-Ribble PD2s were converted into tow wagons. The Leopards and Worldmasters together with the Tiger Cub and PD3 remained in service for several years, the last being sold in 1975. Nowadays Midland Bluebird still works into Coatbridge but neither the buses nor the town itself bear any resemblance to their predecessors. For a bout of nostalgia we have to dip into the photograph album.

Left:
In 1960 Highland bought a new Leyland Tiger Cub coach. It had a Duple (Midland) body and when new ran in overall cream. It was later painted cream and red.

Below left:
Highland's double-deckers were generally second-hand Titans, which made the purchase of a brand-new PD3 all the more surprising. It was bought from dealer stock in 1962 for use on a town service in Cumbernauld and had a 72-seat Alexander body of a type then being supplied to Glasgow Corporation.

Below:
Between 1961 and 1964 six new L1 Leopard buses joined the Highland fleet. The first two had Alexander bodies, one of which is seen leaving Coatbridge for Moodiesburn in 1964.

The average age of the fleet in 1966 was over 11 years. The only buses to be repainted into Alexander (Midland) livery were the Aberdonians, the PD3, the Tiger Cub and the five Worldmasters and six Leopards.

Above:
Alexander (Midland) retained Highland's Greenfoot garage until the completion of a new depot in Cumbernauld. Seen at Greenfoot in the summer of 1967 are, from the left, a 1961 Leopard/Alexander; an ex-Ribble PD2; and an ex-Glasgow Corporation Leyland Worldmaster. The Titan is still in Highland red; the two single-deckers are in Midland livery.

Below:
The end: a Scottish Aviation-bodied Valkyrie.

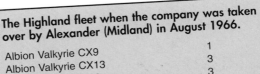

The Highland fleet when the company was taken over by Alexander (Midland) in August 1966.

Albion Valkyrie CX9	1
Albion Valkyrie CX13	3
Albion Valiant CX39	3
Albion Victor FT39	1
Albion Aberdonian MR11	2
Leyland Tiger PS1	1
Leyland Tiger PS2	2
Leyland Titan PD1	1
Leyland Titan PD2	3
Leyland Titan PD3	1
Leyland Worldmaster	5
Leyland Tiger Cub	1
Leyland Leopard L1	6
Total	30